The 3 Dimensions *of* Emotions

The 3
Dimensions
of
Emotions

Finding the Balance of Power, Heart, and
Mindfulness in All of Your Relationships

Dr. Sam Alibrando

New Page Books
A division of The Career Press, Inc.
Wayne, N.J.

THE 3 DIMENSIONS OF EMOTIONS
EDITED BY PATRICIA KOT
TYPESET BY KARA KUMPEL
Original cover design by Jeff Piasky
Triangle illustration by Yuriy Vlasenko/shutterstock
Hands image by happydancing/shutterstock
Printed in the U.S.A.

To order this title, please call toll-free 1-800-CAREER-1 (NJ and Canada: 201-848-0310) to order using VISA or MasterCard, or for further information on books from Career Press.

The Career Press, Inc.
12 Parish Drive
Wayne, NJ 07470
www.careerpress.com
www.newpagebooks.com

Library of Congress Cataloging-in-Publication Data

CIP Data Available Upon Request.

Acknowledgments

I want to thank Gina Stepp, MA, who helped me make a conceptual book more readable. She brought her combined ability to write (and edit) and her professional knowledge of human growth and change to bear. She's been a great encouragement to me. I want to thank the numerous clients—both clinical and corporate—who thought through and lived through the ins-and-outs of the model with me as we applied these concepts in viable practice with real results. I want to thank all the people who took time out of their busy schedule to write a review and/or endorsement. I would like to thank my literary agent, Linda Langton, for all her hard work and dedication in finding such a great publisher for my book. I want to thank my two children, Samantha and JD, who helped me to do research for the book. But more than anyone, I want to thank my beloved wife, Janette, who stood by me for so many years as I labored over the content and then its writing. I left her alone way too much. But more than anything, she challenged me to live the principles in the book and not just write about them. I am a better man for her.

Contents

Preface

11

Chapter 1: Reactivity and Responsibility

17

Chapter 2: The 3 Dimensions of the
Interpersonal World

51

Chapter 3: Working the Triangle

79

Chapter 4: Moving Against and the Power Dimension

105

Chapter 5: Moving Toward and the Heart Dimension

133

Chapter 6: Moving Away and the Mindfulness
Dimension
169

Chapter 7: Synergy and Finding Balance
in All Our Relationships
199

Conclusion
233

Notes
235

Index
243

Preface

This book is born after more than 30 years of labor. The model in this book was conceived when I was a young man in graduate school. Over the years the ideas in this book gestated, developed, and matured. I've used the model in my work with countless clinical clients, organizational clients, and students over the decades. Their engagement with the process helped me refine the ideas to the point that I've presented it in numerous workshops and written about it in various articles and blogs, and introduced it in a previous book, *Follow the Yellow Brick Road: How to Change for*

the Better When Life Gives You its Worst. I've incorporated several grand concepts of many thought leaders
to enrich and deepen the ideas in the book. And most
of all, it is a by-product of itself. In other words, it took
the ongoing balance of Power (a lot of hard work, confidence, determination, and perseverance), Heart (a
great deal of love and passion), and Mindfulness (reflection and deep considerations and at times "not-
knowing") to bring it to term.

The ideas in this book are profound, but not because they are mine. They are *not* mine. I merely pack-
aged several theories into (I hope) a coherent whole
and then made it practical. If there is anything unique
in the model it is the concept of how it can be applied
in our lives. That aspect provides a road map that can
guide us to move from negative, ineffective (if not destructive) reactivity to a more positive, stable, and dynamic response-ability. It can be used in the here and
now—when you are on the verge of "losing it"—and it
can be also a way of life that keeps us on the "road less
traveled," the narrow path of personal growth.

The concepts in the book work in any and all of
our relationships. So whether you are the CEO of a
Fortune 500 corporation or its janitor, a leader of a work
group or its member, a sixth-grade teacher or student,
a psychotherapist working with a difficult client or the
difficult client, a couple trying to work through an argument, or a parent of a challenging teenager, these
principles can help guide you. The model applies not
only to individuals, but in so many ways to groups as
well—families, work teams, sports teams, religious

groups, nations, and even Congress. If practiced, the ideas in this book can change the way you live your life as well as the way we all—collectively—live our lives.

This book is about the three dimensions of being human. In a narrow sense, it is about emotional intelligence, the capacity to know and manage our *self* as well as our emotions, and to know and "manage" others in our lives. In a broad sense it is about emotion—if by emotion we mean the psychosocial-emotional part of each of us that interacts with the psychosocial-emotional part of others. In fact, I considered titling it *eMotion* because it is a study of the three dimensions in which we psychologically, relationally, and emotionally move.

A word about confidentiality is in order. Many of the examples in this book come from 35 years of work as a psychotherapist, an organizational consultant, an executive director (of a training clinic), and as a graduate school instructor. I frequently illustrate the book's concepts by using examples of people that I meet in these various roles. However, I go out of my way to change the names, situations, and gender of the individuals involved in order to protect any and all identities—sometimes blending two or more people or situations into one example. Any similarities to someone you may know is unintentional and coincidental.

This is my baby, lovingly presented to you. This is my small contribution to a grand endeavor shared by many people dedicated to changing the world, as we know it, into a better space where each of us is free to become our truest and best self because we have found the balance of personal Power, Heart, and Mindfulness. Enjoy!

I invite all purchasers of this book to take the Interpersonal Triangle Inventory (ITI). You can use the results of this inventory to see where you might fit (chapters 1 and 2) and what movement you need to integrate (Chapter 3). To take this free inventory (preferably before you start to read the book), go to *www.power-heart-mindfulness.com*, sign in, and download the ITI.

Chapter 1
Reactivity and Responsibility

*No problem can be solved from the same
level of consciousness that created it.*
Albert Einstein

There is a serious obstacle that we each have to face and transcend in order to find true joy and success in living: our *self.* The greatest obstacle to your happiness—I am sorry to tell you—is not your spouse. The greatest obstacle to your happiness is not your boss, your employees, your mother, the economy, or the president of the United States. The greatest obstacle to your happiness and success is you.

You might be saying to yourself at this point, "Wow, what a negative way to start a book!" However, it is actually good news because the truth is we have little or no control over those people and things outside of us to which we often attribute our happiness. There are so many things that affect us that we cannot control: the country where we were born, the mental health of our parents, what genes we inherited, what wealth we inherited, the personality of our spouse (that we did not notice when we were dating), the leadership abilities of our boss, the Congress we (or they) elected, and the myriad things that happen to us every day. The real issue of how we live our life as adults does not come down to what happens to us. The real issue of how we live our life, eventually and essentially, comes down to how we personally *respond* to what happens to us.

Do you ever wonder how certain people who have gone through a serious tragedy can still be happy? I think of celebrities like Christopher Reeve or Michael J. Fox, who seemingly found a way to be happy in spite of serious physical challenges. Sometimes people who suffer major life setbacks suggest that they are even happier after the tragedy! The secret in these situations—big or small—depends on how people are able to respond to life, not what happens to them.

My daughter went to work with the indigenous people in Guatemala. Guatemala is one of the poorest countries in the Americas, and she went to the poorest villages in the country. She told me something our

American minds can hardly comprehend. In spite of all the poverty that they lived in, the villagers were happy. In spite of not owning a nice car or the newest electronic gadget, huge smiles came easily and often to their faces. Our happiness exists not in the outside world but between our ears (and in our heart). This is easy for me to say, but it is a long and continuous journey for me to live.

In all honesty, I spent most of my life subtly resisting this idea. Oh sure, I gave it lip service. After all, I am a well-read psychologist. But like most people, and with true sincerity, I too often lived as if my happiness depended on other people and other things (like status, money, youth, etc.). I preached personal responsibility from the pulpit of my clinical office and from the lectern in boardrooms and workshops. But inside, I lived otherwise. It was only after a lot of therapy, endless "discussions" with my wise wife, and exposure to compelling spiritual wisdom that I began to slowly change my *mind*—not just my intellect—and as a result gradually find happiness that I did not enjoy before. When I embrace this truth of personal happiness through personal responsibility, I transcend all the petty envies and experience wholeness and joy. I invite you to do the same.

Scratch Without an Itch

If the problem does not start with ourselves—and it often does—the solution almost always *ends* with us. The more I grasp and embody this idea, strangely, the happier and more content I become. When I observe my wife, my clients, and even on occasion my govern-ment embrace personal responsibility, things eventu-ally change for the better.

I want you to know that when I use the term *re-sponsibility*, I have a very specific definition. When I use this term, it goes beyond the moral imperatives and duty that we learned when we were kids. ("It's your responsibility to clean your room!") From my per-spective, responsibility is the *ability* to *respond* instead of reacting.

When we are confronted with challenges in life, we can either react with knee-jerk negative attitudes and behaviors, or we can respond with Personal Power, Heart, and Mindfulness. This distinction makes all the difference in how we live our life and how we im-pact others around us. It determines whether we are effective, happy, and well.

This book is about how to develop response-abil-ity—or the ability to respond. It's a concept we have been hearing about for a few thousand years (from Buddha, Moses, Jesus, Mohammed, and many other spiritual teachers), but we still have so much more to learn and un-learn. I join with others who believe that the world is on the cusp of important changes in this area and that there is a dynamic shift just around the corner.

A few years ago I had the opportunity to visit Florence, Italy, the birthplace of the Renaissance. The Renaissance was a time of elemental upheaval and a great awakening in Western culture; the world has not been the same since. Perhaps we are on the verge of a new renaissance, one that is psychological and spiritual in nature. I am not talking here about formal "religion." Too often formal religion takes fresh, life-giving principles and codifies these teachings into fear-based rules that bind people rather than freeing them. No, I am talking about transcendence, where true psychology marries dynamic spirituality to yield a better human being.

How Would You React?

THE SCENE: You hear that one of your employees was late for a meeting with a very important client. A great deal was riding on the meeting, and the employee had a critical role to play in the agenda. This is not the first time that he has been late. He tells everyone that his child was sick, and he had to find someone to watch her. Things went poorly in the meeting, to a great degree because of his lateness and lack of preparation. You receive a call from your partner questioning you about your employee's performance and then you run into the employee in an empty hallway outside your office a few minutes after the call from your partner.

What would *you* do at that moment? How would *you* react when you see him?

This is not a trick question. This is real life. I could have picked an example of a disagreement at home with a child or perhaps a dispute with a neighbor or a challenge you have with one of your parents. I could have described a standoff between two political parties on an important bill, two countries over trade practices, or two churches over homosexuality. This is where we live—whether on an individual, organizational, or national level. How well we navigate these types of challenges determines how well we live.

So, how would you react to your employee?

There are three primary ways that we react to an interpersonal challenge. They are the negative manifestations of the three relational dimensions that we will discuss in Chapter 2. They are the same three ways that organisms use to protect themselves: Fight, Flight, and Freeze/Appease. For now let's simply use the primary colors—Red, Yellow, and Blue—to label the three *primary* ways people react.

Let's use –Red for the negative side of the aggressive or *Fight* reaction. In the –Red bucket we have angry behaviors like:

- ⋏ Hostility and arguing;
- ⋏ Criticizing, blaming, or even attacking; and
- ⋏ Losing one's temper and impatience.

In the scene above, a person reacting –Red would reprimand the employee, possibly firing him on the spot. A person reacting –Red would *stop* his employee and put him in his place. The employee's excuse about his child is one too many, and his boss has run out of patience.

–Yellow will represent the avoidant or *Flight* reaction. In the –Yellow bucket we have detached reactions like:

⅄ Emotional disconnect,

⅄ Evasion and withdrawal, and

⅄ Not acting and putting off.

In the scene above, a person reacting −Yellow, might, with eyes to the floor, walk past the employee. He'll let it go this time, not knowing what to say; perhaps he will talk to him later. Why make a scene now until all the facts are gathered? (Actually, why make a scene at all?)

And finally, −Blue represents the adapting or *Freeze/Appease* reaction. In the −Blue bucket we have compliant reactions like:

⅄ Abdicating and yielding appeasing,

⅄ Conforming and agreeing; and

⅄ Surrendering, giving up, and resigning.

In the scene above, a boss acting −Blue would gingerly question the employee about being late for the important meeting. Upon hearing about the sick child and the difficult situation his employee found himself in that morning, −Blue would adapt to the employee's perspective and consequently excuse him and even feel sorry for the concerned father.

Take a moment to reflect. If you were the boss, out of what paint bucket (or two) would you be tempted to paint/react?

Let's try an example from the home front.

You are at a public event with your spouse. Being the extrovert that he is, your spouse gets notably involved in being part of the "scene" and as a result you are left out a good deal of the time. As you are driving home with him in the car, you say with a hint of upset in your voice, "You ignored me almost the entire evening." He reacts by becoming emotionally distant and distracts himself with the new app on his phone. He could easily spend the rest of the trip home mutely fidgeting with the technology in the hope a disagreement could be averted. How would you be tempted to react? You are likely to *feel* the two-sided coin of hurt and anger, but how do you *behave*?

If you react out of the −Red bucket of behaviors you are likely to become angry and verbally aggressive. You had no patience for this behavior at the event and even less patience for the withdrawal from you now. You lay into him with a barrage of criticism and blame. You give him a full accounting of all the other times that he has treated you this way. You tell him that you are fed up and will be damned if you'll take it any longer.

If you reacted from the −Blue bucket of behaviors you would, upon seeing that you caused him discomfort by your confrontation, feel badly for putting him in an awkward spot. Perhaps you would sympathize with him in an attempt to be fair, adopting his point of view (while losing yours). So you'd begin to engage in nonthreatening dialogue, perhaps asking him about the new app and taking an interest in what he is doing. His bad feelings are now good feelings. Mission accomplished.

You can always paint from the –Yellow bucket of behaviors. After all, that's the bucket he chose in his reaction to you. When you confronted him about his behavior, he became detached and quiet. He turned off, tuned out, and went away. You could do the same. You could become quiet, sullen, and distracted, and go into your own thoughts, perhaps fidgeting with the radio or checking in on the kids. In any case, it would be a very quiet ride home.

How would *you* react if this were your spouse? You might start out with the –Red paint bucket and stick to it, yelling at him all the way home. You might try one set of reactions and then switch to another if the first one does not work—and it generally does not. For example, you might first start by criticizing him and when that does not seem to work, switch to the –Yellow paint bucket by "giving up" and detaching. Either way, you would find yourself frustrated, having to suffer this most difficult person.

The world is full of difficult people. There are the likes of the aforementioned employee and spouse. There are countless difficult bosses, coworkers, children, neighbors, in-laws, partners, teachers, political parties, religious groups, and nations. We react to them in hate out of the –Red bucket, abdication in the –Blue bucket, and indifference and detachment in the –Yellow bucket. Out of fear and threat, consciously or subconsciously, we do react, but who are these difficult people?

The Myth of Difficult People

A woman came into my office for the first time and told me the following story. While in a grocery store, shopping for family provisions, she accidentally and painfully ran over her toe with a heavily laden shopping cart. She yelled, under her breath in the store, at her husband, "You idiot!" She told me in our interview that it was at that moment that she knew it was time to come in for help. She realized with much embarrassment that not only did her husband not hurt her big toe, he wasn't even in the store.

It's a funny story, but not too far from experiences we have all had, when we have readily blamed someone (often our spouse) for our unhappiness. In the part of the mind where most of us live out our lives—the *unconscious limbic system*—the problem becomes the other person. But as we can clearly see from this example, in truth there is often no need to blame anyone. Indeed, laying blame does not effectively solve *most* of our differences with others.

One of my first goals when facilitating a workshop on the topic of managing difficult people is to dispel the very myth of the difficult person. The difficulty with the concept of a "difficult person" is establishing exactly who the difficult person is. We almost always experience the *other* person as difficult. In the case of the woman in the grocery store, she saw her husband as the difficult person.

Often when facilitating this topic at a workshop, I will ask the participants a simple question: "Is 50°F cold or hot?" I almost always get the same response:

"It depends," and so it does. If you were at an outdoor dinner party in Los Angeles in July, 50°F would be very chilly. If you were in Chicago in February, you would be enjoying a welcome warm spell. I use this to illustrate the subjectivity involved when we identify someone as the difficult person. Is the problem the other person or am I the problem? The question might be as subjective as "Is it cold or hot?" Often from our perspective, we only see the other person as difficult.

I define a "difficult person" as anyone who makes *us* into a difficult person. In other words, anyone who "makes us" react. Otherwise, the person or the situation is just a challenge that we need to handle. You have more than likely heard a realtor saying, "What are the three most important things to consider in buying a property?" The answer is: "location, location, location!" Similarly, the first three principles of managing "difficult people" are equally compelling. In order to manage a so-called "difficult person," you must:

1. Manage yourself first,
2. Manage yourself first, and (yes, you guessed it)
3. Manage yourself first!

There are a few good reasons for this. First and foremost, we only have actual control over ourselves. In reality we only have access to our own steering wheel, gas pedal, and brake: If we tried to drive another person's car from the passenger's side we would in all likelihood cause an accident. Second, when we change ourselves and respond positively, we actually change the interpersonal dynamic of the interaction. When *we* are different, the dynamics of the interaction change. Finally, managing yourself first is simply the right thing to do. It is a generally accepted principle in our society that a person of integrity is a person who takes responsibility for his or her own actions. Blaming not only does not work, it is unflattering to the blamer. It is hard to respect a person who is constantly making up excuses and blaming others for their woes and poor behavior. On the other hand, we honor a person who stands up and takes responsibility for their side of the equation. Think of politicians who constantly take credit for what goes right and blame the other party for everything that goes wrong. How much respect does that engender among voters?

I have worked in the field of psychology for more than 35 years. When I think of the ingredients that go into positive change and growth—whether at home or at work—one attribute keeps coming to the top of my list: It is the ability and willingness to own our own "stuff," without excuses and without shame. It is the shameless ownership of our side of the equation. It is the non-arrogant acceptance of who we are, the whole package, embracing our strengths and weaknesses. It is the fierce emotional honesty that we can have with ourselves without self-hate.

People who are humbly self-aware are people who change. Within a relatively short period of time, I can often tell if the couple that comes in to see me to "save their marriage" or the CEO who wants to "fix her executive team" will be successful. If each spouse or the CEO can accept their part in the problem, there is hope. If they are intractably attributing the problem to the other (–Red), see themselves as victims (–Blue), or are passive and indifferent (–Yellow), then we will have our work cut out for us. In these situations, perhaps a Band-Aid solution is all we can hope for.

Only a few of us naturally and easily accept who we are without self-hate and/or blaming others. Most of us, myself included, have to eventually get to this point of true and humble self-awareness *and* self-acceptance through trials and tribulations. There are people who are so insecure that they seldom own their part in *any* problem. To them it is always and only someone and something else. I am not advocating mindless confession to crimes not committed, but the acknowledgment of one's own contribution. It is seldom entirely one person's fault, and it almost always takes two to keep the problem going.

In order to successfully manage the many and unavoidable interpersonal challenges—previously referred to as *difficult people*—we start and perhaps end with our responsibility. Or, if you will, response-ability. You see, the problem essentially comes down to first managing our own reactivity.

For the most part, the *difficult person* becomes "difficult" (to us) when *we* become reactive. Now let's face it: There are times when the other person, truly and only, is problematic. There are also other times when, without doubt, *we* are at fault. Yet most of the time, it is a complex subjective interaction between two emotionally charged, reactive people. However, we only have the steering wheel, brake, and gas pedal for our side of the drive. The key, therefore, is to learn how to drive responsibly.

Before we go to the solution, let's understand the problem better. That will make the solution even more clear.

The Ego and Pain-Body

I looked up synonyms for the word *reactivity*. The synonyms fell generally into one of three clusters:

- ⋏ Behavior that is a reply or rejoinder to another behavior ← Comeback
- ⋏ Hasty, knee-jerk, impetuous, sudden ← Abrupt
- ⋏ Without thought, forethought or judgment; unwise ← Unthinking

So when we are reactive there is a somewhat abrupt, unthinking comeback to someone or something. We counter another's behavior or attitude (real or imagined) with one that is hasty and impulsive. The outcome of such reactive behaviors is at best worthless and at worst downright harmful. Sometimes the reactivity lasts only a few seconds, and sometimes the reaction become stuck in our "psyche" for the rest of our life.

Melinda was still affected by Mike's affair even though it had happened more than a decade before. They were watching their favorite show on TV when a lingerie commercial popped up. What happened next happened quickly. Mike's eyes opened slightly to the images on the screen. Melinda exclaimed, "I saw you looking at that woman! Do you want to sleep with her, too?" Mike stammered and grunted defensively. Busted . . . but for what? His mind froze, caught someplace between guilt and fear. What could he possibly say? All he wanted to be was somewhere else. His inarticulate retort and evasive disposition only made Melinda angrier and re-injured, as if the affair had happened the previous week.

For the next few hours, two people exchanged pain until thoroughly exhausted. Worn out, Melinda finally retreated and Mike was released from the corner in which he was trapped. Any love, peace, or positive feelings that started the evening had evaporated, annihilated by reactivated memories. *Reactivity kills liveliness.*

Peter was a "nice" boss. When it became clear that he had to confront one of the people who worked for him, his body tightened, and his mind became tense. He summoned enough courage to call the employee into his office. He had reviewed the script in his head several dozen times and once on a piece of paper. The issue was clear, the problem compelling. Yet when the employee exited his office a few minutes later, the employee was excused without conditions. The employee's presence and meager excuse trumped all that had been compelling only 10 minutes before. Without knowing it, Peter adopted and adapted to the employee's way of thinking. After she left, Peter stared at his talking points on the piece of paper wondering what had happened, then numbly reached for the phone to make the next call on his to-do list. *Reactivity causes one to lose oneself.*

In each of these examples, Melinda, Mike (Melinda's husband), and Peter all reacted—albeit in different ways. What they had in common was that they were reacting rather than responding.

In the beginning of the chapter we talked about the three general categories—or paint buckets—of how we react. Each of these reactions—Red, Blue, or Yellow—has at its basis the impulse to protect the self. This Protector within us has a name: *Ego.*

By Ego, I mean the part of the mind that is mindlessly bent on defending its sense of *self* and *significance,* often at the expense of others, reality, and, in a paradoxical way, its host (the individual). Although well intended from its narrow perspective, our Ego often gets us into trouble. In fact, most, if not every offense taken has as its origin an injured Ego. Wounded Egos are the source of intractable negotiations, lost love, enemies made, and wars started. A sensitive or excited Ego is, by definition, *reactive.*

Related to the Ego is the idea of *pain-body.* Eckhart Tolle developed the idea of pain-body in his book *A New Earth: Awakening to Your Life's Purpose.*[1] Painbody, as I understand it, is the accumulation of all the pain and suffering we have endured and internalized, both directly in our formative experiences and also indirectly from what we inherited or "downloaded" from our family and the various cultures we swam in. More specifically, it is made up of pain and suffering that we internalized that was not consciously processed at the time of its cause either by ourselves or with the help of another, such as a parent or nanny.

The mind accumulates, collates, and then stores emotionally charged themes—or as I like to call them *emotion–notions*. This is what I believe Eckhart Tolle refers to as pain-body. The old psychoanalysts call these "unintegrated psychological entities" *introjects*.[2] Some neuroscientists call these unintegrated psychological entities "emotional memories or implicit memories." In a previous book, I used the character from L. Frank Baum's *The Wonderful Wizard of Oz*, the Wicked Witch of the West, to represent those unintegrated painful and scary parts of us.[3] No matter what you call them, if they never get properly *metabolized*, they stay in us as *unintegrated psychological entities*, as if they have a life of their own inside our minds. The following excerpt is from an article written by Eckhart Tolle about the pain-body:

> This accumulated pain is a negative energy field that occupies your body and mind. If you look on it as an invisible entity in its own right, you are getting quite close to the truth. It's the emotional pain-body. It has two modes of being: dormant and active. . . . The pain-body wants to survive, just like every other entity in existence, and it can only survive if it gets you to unconsciously identify with it. It can then rise up, take you over, "become you," and live through you. It needs to get its "food" through you. It will feed on any experience that resonates with its own kind of energy, anything that creates further

pain in whatever form: anger, destructiveness, hatred, grief, emotional drama, violence, and even illness. So the pain-body, when it has taken you over, will create a situation in your life that reflects back its own energy frequency for it to feed on. Pain can only feed on pain. Pain cannot feed on joy. It finds it quite indigestible.[4]

If this is not a description of a "demon" that "possesses" us, I don't know what is. In fact some (nonreligious) psychological theorists refer to these unintegrated psycho-emotional entities as "daemons."[5] I find it fascinating that the same term, *daemon*, is used by computer programmers for programs that run behind the scenes in a computer. We don't ever see these programs working like we would our e-mail or word processor but they are there. We call daemons that are written for malicious purposes, computer *viruses*. As metaphors go, I like to use the biological version of viruses as an analogy of how the pain-body works. Viruses are foreign entities that take over the natural functioning of our cells to do as they wish. Viruses are in our body but not *of* our body, often dormant until activated by some external stimuli or condition. Just think of a fever blister, a virus on your lip that erupts after being in the sun too long. Likewise, psychological viruses—our pain-bodies based on our more adverse emotion–notions—can stay dormant until some "difficult person" or situation triggers them, and then the psycho-emotional eruption takes place. Not too far away from this outbreak is an injured or threatened

Ego. The puss from this viral outbreak can show up in any blend of three primary colors: Red, Blue, or Yellow.

Melinda's pain-body was inflamed in the color Red. The mere perception of her husband being tantalized by another woman activated an intense emotional memory—as if he had just cheated on her. Her pain-body, her unmetabolized set of emotion–notions accumulated over all the times she had felt betrayed and unloved, was triggered. Her Ego went into action to "protect and to defend." She hated this man across from her as if he were every man who had ever hurt her. Her pain-body was activated, as her Ego strove to protect itself at all costs.

In a Red reaction, the protective Ego fights; it is engaged as the aggressor. It intends to hurt rather than be hurt. It seeks revenge. It takes no prisoners. It blames. It has no guile to own, but only offense to be taken. The inflamed pain-body corresponds (literally co-responds or reacts) with the Ego. They are a tag team, if not versions of the same psychological "thing." A pain-body inflamed in the color Red is a blaming, mean, and angry pain-body.

Mike's reaction was different. His reaction was mostly Yellow. When he was confronted with his wife's anger, he went offline. He was overwhelmed. He could no longer think or feel his way out of the pain and into a healthy space. He detached. He only wanted to get away. For the next hour his body stayed in the room (the torture chamber), but his mind, if not his soul, had already left.

The Ego, in this case, protects itself by leaving the scene of the crime. Unlike the Ego in the color of Red, the Yellow reaction is not to fight but to flee. This is a common process for children who endure overwhelming verbal, physical, or sexual abuse. Their body stays but every other part of them leaves. What other option do they have? They cannot fight the powerful antagonist, and often the antagonist is the very same person who is appointed to take care of them. Thus, they endure by leaving psychologically until they can leave physically. We call this psychological defense, *dissociation*. It allows the mind to distance itself from experiences that are too much for the psyche to process at the time.

Mike's accumulation of emotion–notions had supported a pain-body that tended to drive him toward a flight response, and in this case, it was activated in reaction to his wife. In truth, there was no real threat to Mike. His wife was angry with him, that's all. He had been faithful to her since the initial and only affair. She was not going to harm him physically and if she tried—short of a sharp object or gun—he could easily handle her. There was no real threat. Yet he reacted as if he had just been caught for the first time. His pain-body remembers; he has no defense against its power. His pain-body erupts with feelings that cannot be endured, so the emotional circuit breaker pops, the fuse blows, and the Ego takes over. If no one else will protect him, his Ego will.

A word about pain-bodies activating other pain-bodies is in order. Human beings—like dogs, our beloved best friends—are pack animals. As a result, we have developed a keen sense of inter-group communication that is only in a small part verbal. For better or for worse, our emotional brain triggers or activates another's emotional brain. You know this phenomenon if you have ever been to a comedy club. Laughter is contagious. Everyone's funny bone getting tickled tickles everyone else's funny bone. What sounds like an average joke when you're sitting at home in front of the TV becomes a knee-slapping, tear-jerking, can't-breathe caliber joke in a live audience (or pack) of people. Likewise, when a pain-bodied Ego gets stirred up, it often activates another's pain-body and Ego as well. In his book *Primal Leadership,* Daniel Goleman considered this phenomenon with leaders. He found that only a small part of effective (and ineffective) leadership is verbal. For good or ill, the leader's emotional brain powerfully impacts those that he or she leads. This is what happened to Melinda and Mike, and it can happen to any of us in our most important relationships at home and work. This is what can happen in our kitchen, a boardroom, at a kid's soccer game, in the Congress of the United States, and between religious congregations. This is also what happened to Peter.

Just as Melinda and Mike reacted to one another, Peter reacted to his errant employee; and he reacted in the color of Blue. Where Reds react with fight and Yellows with flight, Blues adapt. In fact, they over-adapt. They freeze and appease, they conform so as not to make themselves a threat. The Blue's Ego defends itself by being good, but without taking into account its truest good. Because the Ego's purpose is to protect its host's sense of safety and importance, when the Blue gives up, yields, and adapts to the other's way of thinking, he does it for protection. When Mona, my 23-pound dog, gets around Terra, her 45-pound girl-friend, she will often roll over onto her back, exposing her stomach to Terra. This signals to Terra that Mona is submitting so Terra won't hurt her. Mona is dipping into the Blue paint bucket of behaviors.

Peter is a very nice man, too nice for his own good and his company's benefit. Peter anticipated what was inevitable, a different story from the employee, so he wrote down what he wanted to say. It failed to help him. The employee was offended; she had a "good rea-son" for her behavior and at once Peter saw it from her point of view. The talking points on his scrap paper soon became blurry ink. Peter backed down. For a moment he felt "understanding" and "important" for being the better man, the "empathic boss." However, the employee left without consequence, while Peter was left frozen—like a rusted Tin Man in the forest.

No doubt his pain-body was activated. Perhaps it arose from emotion–notions formed when he was a boy while experiencing a domineering father. Perhaps the only way to survive was to adapt, and the only way to adapt was to blend into the way Father saw the world. His Ego would likely have protected him by rolling him over on his back, rendering him nonthreatening and agreeable. Perhaps he also developed a sense of great importance by being his mother's little champion because, unlike her "evil" husband—his father, young Peter showed he understood her. He would likely have maintained this sense of importance as an adult by not being "the bad guy" but being the "understanding and likeable" boss. Peter's emotion–notions fed a pain-bodied reaction that was neither Red's fight nor Yellow's flight, but Blue's freeze and appease.

L.I.A.R, L.I.A.R. Pants on Fire

Okay, if we human beings are so smart why can't we control our reactivity? If we can do open-heart surgery, run 26 miles in relatively short periods of time, make powerful computers that we carry around in our pocket, think through complex mathematical and philosophical problems, why in the world can't we control ourselves? If we ever hope to have a better world, this is very important question to answer. The last frontier for great human accomplishments is not in the vast ocean or outer space, but in "inner space."

Both my clinical and business clients often comment on how calm (non-reactive) they find me. And in truth, I am calm and fairly non-reactive . . . with them. Just don't ask my family what I am like when I am trying to get to the airport on time or when my computer is not working the way technology intended. It is easy to be calm when our pain-body is dormant and the Ego is not threatened. However, all of us at some time—and some of us often—have pain-body eruptions. I don't believe for a moment that anyone is free from unproductive—if not harmful—reactivity. I do not know of any groups (corporations, political parties, religious groups, yes, even nonprofit organizations) that are immune to the woes of reactivity. We *all* have emotion–notions accumulated from our life expe-riences, and as a result we all can and will react out of our resulting pain-body.

Any of us with any semblance of honesty and self-awareness can't help wonder at times, "Why did I react like that?" That is the question: "Why do we all—at some time—react in ways that don't make sense and have negative outcomes?" Organizational research is compelling and has indicated that positive, engaged styles of management yield the most productivity out of employees. Why do managers still use anger and in-timidation to "motivate" workers? When has calling your husband a name or neglecting your wife emotion-ally ever built a more fulfilling relationship? Yet we still do it. We know that constant criticism of children has a negative impact that will stay with them throughout their life, so why do we still mindlessly criticize them? Why?

Blame it on the Brain

There is an acronym that I use to depict the nature of our reactivity and its intractable place in our lives: L.I.A.R.

- ⋏ Limbic.
- ⋏ Intense.
- ⋏ Automatic.
- ⋏ Resistant.

Limbic

In large part, our reactivity is generated by and originates in our emotional brain, the limbic system. Nestled somewhere between our brain stem and our cortex lies the culprit. During workshops, I invite participants to put a finger just above their ear and then the other finger at the bridge of their nose, between their eyes. I then say, "Where the fingers intersect, deep within your brain, is the limbic system." Every time we enjoy the company of a friend or lover, are transported listening to a piece written by Bach, or take pleasure in a delicious meal or a sexual experience, the limbic system is there making the experience . . . well, an experience. It is from within the limbic system that we protect ourselves from *real* threats that confront us. When a wild animal confronted our ancestors, the limbic system would kick in to both compel and propel us to run or fight, before we had the time or luxury to think about it. The important thing to know about the limbic system is that it not only is part of what we call the "mind," but it also has a mind of its own. In other words, we have little control over what *initially* happens in the limbic system because it is by nature reactive.

When discussing L.I.A.R. during workshops, I will often do a special trick. I will wave the index finger on my right hand and make my entire left arm rise and then descend. At this point the audience looks at me like I am an idiot. Of course you can make your left arm rise and fall at will. Then I challenge them to do that with their emotions. Can you wave your index finger—on either hand—and make yourself more or less angry, happy, sad, bad, or scared? Unless you are a gifted actor, of course you can't. That is the difference between the cortex and the limbic system; we have relatively little control over our reactive, emotional mid-brain.

Another aspect of the limbic brain is that there is no real concept of time—as we otherwise experience time—so when an emotional memory gets activated it does not register as a memory per se. Melinda did not say to herself (nor to Michael), "Oh yeah, this is the very same feeling that I had when I first found out about your affair 12 years ago." No, at that moment it was experienced as an offense happening in the present. When a boss criticizes an employee, the employee doesn't immediately identify all the times his drunken father had said similarly unkind things to him. Because of the limbic system, these emotional memories get reactivated as if they are happening in the present with no real sense of when and from where they originated.

Intense

By nature and design, the limbic system and the emotions it generates can be strong and intense. Sometimes we need strong emotion. I can think of at least two important purposes for emotion. The first purpose of emotion is that it acts as a *signal*. It gets our attention! It is like a warning system that lets us know that something important just happened and the more important it is *perceived* to be, generally the stronger or more intense the signal. For example, you say or do something amiss to someone and then feel "guilty." This *signals* you to either apologize—make things right with them—or to perhaps change future behaviors. Emotions are like the gauge on your car's dashboard letting you know that your oil needs to be changed or that your seat belt is not fastened.

The second value to emotions has to do with *motivation*. Emotion—even as the word suggests—puts us in *motion*. If we are angry we are pushed to fight. If we are in love, we are moved to care for the other. If we are threatened (and are small or outnumbered), emotions energize us to run like hell. So both as a signal and a motivational system, it is necessary that emotions have some degree of intensity—and there seems to be a corresponding intensity of reaction. If we feel miffed, we react by being annoyed. If we are really angry (i.e., enraged) we are tempted to react with hostility.

In order to understand the concept of intensity, it is necessary to explore what I call the *layering effect* or *standing wave*. Arguably, Melinda could have been annoyed a bit by her husband's gaze at another woman, but her reaction was far greater than annoyance. I could be irritated when my computer is not working, but why do I get so upset? The answer can be found in the analogy of a *standing wave*. There is a wonderful example of standing waves in nature: white-water rapids. Here, standing waves in a river occur when one wave "meets" another wave, and the top wave stands on top of the lower wave. They now look like one wave but are as powerful as at least two. In this case, the upper wave, the one that we can see, is the "current"

event (a reaction to a gawking husband or a malfunc-
tioning computer). The wave underneath, perhaps the
larger and more powerful wave, is the *emotional memory*. As a result, we get a reaction of greater amplitude
than we would ordinarily expect.

Emotional memories are not dated along a time line.
They are not experienced as a memory, but as present-
ly occurring events, and as such emotion–notions are
not differentiated from the event that activated them.
Just like a standing wave in a river, emotionally based
reactivity can be of even greater intensity than the
current or original triggering event. Many people walk
about with a huge pain-body of emotion–notions just
waiting for another wave or "current" event—a husband who looks at a sexy woman or a computer that is
not working properly—to trigger an unusually intense
reaction.

Jonathan Haidt has a great metaphor for the limbic
system's intensity. Think of a large, powerful elephant
with a little person sitting atop his neck. As long as the
elephant is calm, this little man can steer the elephant
in any direction he deems necessary for any number of
constructive purposes (to travel, to lift heavy objects,
to go for a Sunday afternoon ride, etc.). However, if the
elephant becomes upset, there is little that the man
can do to control the rampaging animal. The elephant
is the limbic system and the little man is the prefrontal
cortex, where we can choose to make our left arm go
up and down.[6]

We are never more in balance than when our cortex and limbic system work together in concert with

each other, like the little man steering the elephant. However, when we go into a reactive mode, the limbic system can overwhelm the frontal cortex. When this happens it will either cancel out thinking or take it over. For example, when confronted by his wayward employee's excuses, Peter suddenly saw the situation completely from the wayward employee's point of view, forgetting that he had vital and valid reasons to discipline her. His limbic fear of conflict (subtly) overrode his cortical "thinking." For a short period he thought just like she did.

Automatic

The other day I opened a cabinet door in the kitchen. In a flash, I was standing there with a glass in my hand. I hardly remember catching it. When I opened the door a glass fell and without thinking I caught it, automatically. How did I do that? Well, when the nerve impulse from my eyes reached the occipital region of the brain, they split into two directions. The first and faster set of nerves raced to the "lower" brain (brain stem and limbic system), which was quickly ready for action. The second, slower set of nerves went to the cortex, where the event was interpreted and understood based on similar past experiences. To enhance our chances of survival, it's important for the nerve signals headed to the lower brain to get there first; we have to react quickly. A split second can make all the difference between catching a glass and picking up its pieces, or being eaten by a wild animal instead of sticking around to reproduce.

Only a small portion of what we do in our head is accomplished through conscious effort. The rest we perform automatically, without thinking. This is what psychologists call the unconscious or subconscious. It is humbling to know that so much of what we do, perceive, assume, and react to is processed without our conscious consent. It just happens . . . automatically.

Of course, there are "good" automatic reactions, like catching a glass or avoiding an oncoming car. And there are "not-so-good" automatic reactions, like losing your temper or assuming your partner is criticizing you when they are just playing. There are "good" automatic instincts and intuitions based on previously accurate learning, as Malcom Gladwell describes in his book *Blink*.[7] And there are "not-so-good" automatic prejudices that we harbor in spite of all evidence to the contrary. There are "good" automatic habits that we form like personal hygiene and exercise regimes; and there are "not-so-good" automatic habits that we form like using alcohol to avoid feelings. And all of these automatic instincts, intuitions, and habits are . . .

Resistant to Change

Once the brain learns something, it does not like to change. For example, if you decide to improve your tennis game, you take a lesson. The tennis professional suggests a new grip that will improve the accuracy and power of your swing. Even though you trust this stroke will improve your game, you still find yourself going back to the old, less-efficient grip you learned while goofing around in high school. Your brain cries out, "That's not the way we do it around here!" This seems to be true especially when emotional learning is involved. Once a behavior, belief, or emotional disposition gets laid down on the hard drive of our brain, we tend to repeat it and repeat it and repeat it. This is great if you have healthy habits. I, for one, am glad that I do not have to read the owner's manual each night when I brush my teeth. Brushing my teeth, like driving a car or riding a bike, is now second nature.

However, this mechanism is not so good when the things we learn are not adaptive, such as getting angry when we don't get our way or avoiding conflict that requires our attention and response. These habits are not only automatic but they are highly resistant to change.

These four aspects—limbic, intense, automatic, and resistant—together form a highly stable and formidable system. When it is the basis of good behaviors, attitudes, or perceptions, it works very well for everyone. (Think of all the good manners that we routinely display, accidents that we avoid, and glasses that we catch before breaking.) When we automatically respond to people with kindness and understanding, courage and calm resolve, then the default system works well. However, when it forms the basis for negative behaviors, attitudes, and perceptions, we have a problem: a highly dysfunctional system that works well for no one and is not easily changed.

"Just say no" was a phrase made popular by Nancy Reagan. The idea was that kids, when confronted with the opportunity to use drugs, should "just say no" to the temptation. Mrs. Reagan did not have the benefit of all that we now know about the brain. Limbic learning is very powerful, intense, automatic, and highly resistant to change. We have a hard time not reacting in anger when we are criticized (Red), or feeling deeply hurt if someone slights us (Blue), or becoming detached when the sadness of an event is too painful to handle (Yellow). The truth is that it is not always easy to "just say no" when our limbic system is shouting "yes!"

The word translated as "sin" in the Bible comes from the Greek word *hamartia*. It means to miss the mark. When an ancient Greek archer shot his arrow and missed the target, he *sinned*. The word has obviously taken on different meaning over time. For our purposes here, I like the original meaning. Whenever we react rather than respond in a positive constructive way, we miss the mark. We miss our fullest potential. We are off kilter or off balance. We are a people who are capable of great things, not just in the arena of science and technology, but also in the realm of unselfishly caring for others, mounting up courage when confronted with a challenge, and controlling the more "demonic" aspects of our nature.

In this chapter I presented a basic human challenge that we all face: our reactivity to things, events, and especially to other people. Chapter 3 will present a tool—a road map—for moving from destructive reactivity to productive proactivity. But to lay the groundwork, Chapter 2 will introduce you to what I believe to be the "three dimensions of the interpersonal world." I've actually already introduced the three dimensions to you in their reactive form in the three paint buckets, and their characteristics can be summarized as follows:

- ▲ Red is the Power dimension (or height) characterized by Agency.
- ▲ Blue is the Heart dimension (or width) characterized by Empathy.
- ▲ Yellow is the Mind dimension (or depth) characterized by Mindfulness.

Chapter 2 will also introduce you to a model that I call the Interpersonal Triad or Interpersonal Triangle, which is based on the three dimensions and is the basis for the tool that I will present in Chapter 3 to help anyone find their way back into balance. Stay tuned.

If you have not done so yet, using the code that came with the book, go to *www.power-heart-mindfulness.com* and take the *Interpersonal Triangle Inventory* (ITI). You can use the results of this inventory to see where you fit (Chapter 2) and what movement you need to integrate (Chapter 3).

Reflections and Musings

1. We all react in one (or a blend) of the primary paint buckets: Red, Blue, or Yellow. How do you typically react to:

   - ▲ Your spouse, boy/girlfriend, or partner?
   - ▲ Your children?
   - ▲ Your boss or superior?
   - ▲ Your employees?

Did you react to each person the same? If not, why were you different with one rather than the other?

2. What primary colors did your mother display when she reacted when you were a child? And how did you react in return?

3. What primary colors did your father display when he reacted when you were a child? And how did you react in return?

4. Most of the time our pain-body, by its own design, is "invisible," unconscious, and blended into our thinking. How could you tell if and when your pain-body gets activated? What emotion–notions is it based on? What would be the things to look for?

Chapter 2

The 3 Dimensions of the Interpersonal World

[You were not given] . . . a spirit of fear, but a spirit of power, love and a sound mind.
Paul of Tarsus, First Century C.E.

What if you were better able to motivate your work team? What if you were able to respectfully work through a disagreement with your spouse without blame, hurt, or hate? What if you could constructively communicate with your children without losing your cool? Would that make a difference in your life?

Now if you take that vision of healthy relating and expand it to a global scale—congressional leaders calmly and objectively working out differences, world leaders collaboratively solving real issues, and religious leaders holding their own beliefs without hate or prejudice toward those who don't share them—you can imagine the profound change we could experience if we all simply navigated our relationships with grace.

This navigation has a parallel to the physical world. Just as there are three dimensions in the physical world—height, width, and depth—there are also three dimensions in the interpersonal world. I label these three dimensions Power (height), Heart (width), and Mind or Mindfulness (depth). In fact, just as coordination in the physical world helps you to move effectively toward your goals, so, too, coordination in the three dimensions of the interpersonal world helps you to manage your relationships, and thus your own well-being.

Think of people in your life who seem to be exceptional in their ability to relate to you and others. Think hard (perhaps a boss that you once had, a friend from college, a business colleague, or if you are very fortunate, a parent or a spouse). I am willing to wager that they are most often people who are able to move freely and maturely with balance in each of the three dimensions. They are caring and interested and not afraid to admit that they are wrong (the Heart Axis). They are appropriately assertive about what they need or want, and self-respecting (the Power Axis). And they are objective, aware, and even-handed (the Mind Axis).

So what challenges are you facing in your life? Chances are they are interpersonal in nature. You might be in a bad relationship, but you are not able to find the strength to leave it. Or the company you helped start is bogged down by a troublesome partner. Or your parent is still critical of everything you do. Perhaps *you* are the troublesome partner or parent.

If your challenge is not directly personal in nature, there is a great likelihood that relationships will be involved in its resolution. For example, you might have an illness that requires you to confront your doctor who skipped the class on bedside manners in medical school. Perhaps changes in the economy have seriously affected your sales, and you need to motivate your sales team to bring in more business. Think of the difference it would make in these situations if you were able to move freely, with interpersonal limberness. If you are like me, it would make all the difference.

The Interpersonal Triangle

The ideas that form the basis of the three dimensions are not my own. While working toward my master's degree in counseling psychology, I came upon the book *Our Inner Conflicts* by Karen Horney.[1] Horney was a German psychoanalyst who immigrated to the United States in 1930 and is widely known in the psychoanalytic field for her work in anxiety and feminine psychiatry. In *Our Inner Conflicts*, she describes inner conflicts as discrepancies within oneself that are "resolved" or acted out interpersonally in an attempt to alleviate inner tension.

One example of an inner conflict is the classic tension between wanting to exercise your will to get what you want while at the same time not wanting to lose favor with someone. She suggested that we interpersonally "resolve" such a conflict in one of three ways. One way is to employ what she calls a *moving-toward* solution. In this case the conflicted person would re-actively—and often unknowingly—relinquish their needs and desires and instead *adapt* to the other's apparent interests to avoid offending the other person.

In a *moving-against* solution the person does the very opposite. Persuaded by his own perspective and wishes, the person acts "against" the other to control the outcome and get what he wants. Last but not least, in the *moving-away* solution, the person abandons both of the other two strategies and instead avoids, cuts off, shuts down, and checks out.

What captured my interest in Horney's model of human behavior was the simplicity of the three movements. We either move *toward, against,* or *away* from people. I was hard pressed to find situations in which one (or a blend) of these movements could not describe the interpersonal response. As you go through your week, see whether these three ways do not, for the most part, describe the three ways you relationally behave. I think that you will find, as I have, that these three relational positions capture the basic ways we interpersonally move.

I began to use this theory of interpersonal movement in my budding therapy practice and coaching work with individuals and organizations. It turned out to be an extremely effective and practical tool for guiding people through stormy interpersonal challenges and personal growth.

Several years later, while in my doctoral program, I was introduced to the work of Wilfred Bion. Bion is perhaps one of the greatest psychoanalytic minds of the 20th century, but few people—even psychologists—know of him. Among the many notable and creative ideas that he gave to the psychological community are the three ways we emotionally "link" or connect to others: through love, hate, or knowing. I recognized that Bion's triad of emotional linking mapped well with Horney's three emotional movements. *Moving toward* is a lot like Bion's *love*, *moving against* is similar to his *hate*, and *moving away* (becoming truly objective) equates with *knowing* (in the way a scientist understands something). It was at this moment that I recognized the Interpersonal Triad (Triangle).

I began to see the three relational movements in many arenas in life. To help illustrate, let's look at three very different examples.

There is a passage in the New Testament, quoted at the beginning of this chapter, in which Paul advises Timothy about leadership challenges in his church. Paul states that Timothy was "not given a spirit of fear, or anxiety or timidity, but of power (moving against), and of love (moving toward), and of a sound mind (moving away or knowing).[2] Here in one sentence, written 2,000 years ago, Paul has advised his protégé on the elements of the Interpersonal Triangle, whether he knew it or not.

The next example comes from high school biology. There we learn that organisms protect themselves in one of three ways: They fight (move against), take flight (move away), or freeze/appease (move toward). Whether a tiny animal or a world leader, every organism protects itself by fighting, running away, or yielding. In these basic movements of life fundamental to organisms of any size or complexity, we see the Interpersonal Triad. It seems that any organism will protect itself along the same three dimensions.

The final example comes from L. Frank Baum's classic story, one of the most beloved movies of all time, *The Wonderful Wizard of Oz*. One day it dawned on me that Dorothy's three companions each represent one of the three interpersonal movements, or ways of connecting. In each character there is a key element in need of development. The first character, the Scarecrow, needs a brain. The second, a Tin Man, needs a heart. The third, a Lion, needs courage.

Dorothy's companions metaphorically represent the three ways in which we all need to develop: Scarecrow—knowing (moving away, mind, or mindfulness), Tin Man—love (moving toward, heart), and Lion—courage (moving against or power). I felt compelled to share this connection at the next lecture I gave on the three dimensions. After the talk, everyone wanted to talk about Dorothy's three companions. People love the story. They connected with the need to develop within themselves the Scarecrow's mind, the Tin Man's heart, and the Lion's courage. A fellow consultant in the audience challenged me to write an article using the metaphor. It ended up becoming the beginning of a book.

This was the origin of the Interpersonal Triangle. I use a triangle to demonstrate the Interpersonal Triad because it aptly demonstrates both the distinction of the three movements and the fact that they are inexorably and dynamically interconnected.

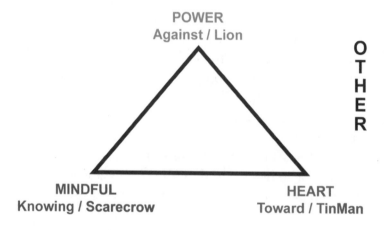

Figure 2.1. The Interpersonal Triangle

Since that time, I have used and taught this model in my clinical practice, in presentations and workshops, and in the coaching and consultancy work I do.

After I wrote my book about Dorothy's three companions and the Interpersonal Triangle, a man called me and probed me with questions about my sources. Eventually satisfied with my answers, he told me that he was the president of a company that produces the

Strength Deployment Inventory (SDI) developed by Dr. Elias Porter.

Little did I know that yet a third psychologist, Porter, had developed the *Relationship Awareness Theory*,[3] which is remarkably similar to Bion's three types of connecting and Horney's three interpersonal movements. In his theory, Porter identified three ways in which people are relationally motivated. There is what he called *Altruistic-Nurturing* motivation, where one is motivated by a concern for others (similar to moving toward, or "love"). There are the *Assertive-Directing* motivations (much like moving against, or "hate"), where one is competing for position of importance or control. And finally, the *Analytic-Autonomizing* motivation (comparable to moving away, or "knowing"), which is motivated by truth, objectivity, and self-control. Apparently, there were other researchers out there who had noticed, defined, and labeled these universal patterns with their own nomenclature.

HORNEY	BION	PORTER	BIOLOGY
Moving Toward	Love	Altruistic	Freeze/ Appease
Moving Against	Hate	Assertive	Fight
Moving Away	Knowing	Analytic	Flight

Table 2.1. Four Sources of the Interpersonal Triangle

The Three Dimensions of the Interpersonal World

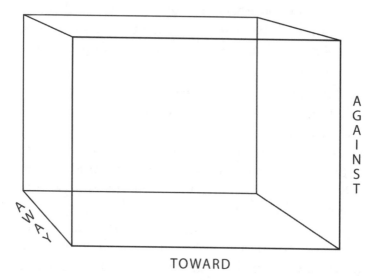

Figure 2.2. The Three Dimensions of the Interpersonal World

The 3 Dimensions of the Interpersonal World

Independent of each other, using different languages and terms, and asking different questions, three highly respected psychologists (and one established biological principle) all arrived at the same juncture. Each pointed to the *Three Dimensions of the Interpersonal World*.

The best way to understand the universality of these movements is to compare them physically and emotionally. In the same way that we move in a physical world of height, width, and length, so do we travel in an interpersonal world. *Toward* is openness to the world of others or width. *Against* is related to the stature that we have in relation to others or height. And *Away* is the distance we have away from others or depth.

We can play with the shape of the cube to depict different "personalities." For example, a person with a forceful, controlling personality—but not warmth—would have proportionately great height (or Against), depicting a cube that looks phallic. Or consider a person who is always giving and often giving up—without much self-regard. They would have proportionally more width or (Toward) without much height (Against), looking a lot like a flat rug—or doormat—on which others can step. Last, we could have someone who is emotionally removed and distant in how they relate—not much warmth or prominence. They would have an exaggerated depth (Away). In this case, the cube would resemble a tunnel with the person far away and inaccessible.

Whenever I present this model to organizations, a percentage of the audience always catches on quite readily. They connect with Horney's terms and can start using them without missing a beat. They say things like "I disagree with what you just said, and therefore I am *moving against*," or "I want to stop and think about that for a while, so I am *moving away*." However, there are also those who do not converse well using these terms. They say things like, "Am I pushing forward now?" or "Would that be pulling

COLOR	HORNEY	BION	PORTER	BIOLOGY	PAUL	BAUM
BLUE	Moving Toward	Love	Altruistic	Freeze/Appease	Love	Tin Man
RED	Moving Against	Hate	Assertive	Fight	Power	Lion
YELLOW	Moving Away	Knowing	Analytic	Flight	Mind	Scarecrow

Table 2.2. The Various Languages for the Three Dimensions of the Interpersonal World

away?" Intelligence has nothing to do with whether or not someone connects with Horney's language. I've had people with genius-level IQs from the California Institute of Technology misunderstand the terms.

To make the terms more accessible and natural for a broader range of people, I have added a color key. I was taught when I was young that there are three primary colors: blue, red, and yellow. And now we know that there are three primary ways we move and connect with others. With this in mind, moving against, the Power dimension, is Red. Red is a color that says stop. Red is often a color of anger, as in the phrase "He made me see red." Yellow is moving away, the Mind dimension. Yellow is the color of caution, of slowing down. Its cousin, gold, is the color of silence and calm, as in the phrase "silence is golden." Finally, Blue represents moving toward, the Heart dimension. Blue reminds me of water and, thus, properties associated with life-giving. It is liquid, moldable, and adaptive. Blue is also used to describe someone who is depressed, as in "I am feeling blue today." And depression is a condition of moving toward where we feel helpless and hopeless.

Now we have the three primary colors matched to three primary ways of relating to others. One of the benefits of using a color code to describe the dimensions and interpersonal movements is that we can blend the colors. Because we do not always act and react in only one dimension, we can often blend dimensions or movements together. For example, if a person is afraid to respond in Red (Power) they are likely to respond in either –Yellow avoidance, –Blue abdication, or a blend of the two, −Green (−Yellow and −Blue blended), peace at any price.

For the most part, throughout this book, I will use color to describe the relational modes and dimensions—with an occasional reference language from these sources and Baum's *Wizard of Oz* characters. I invite you to feel free to substitute any language that works best for you and empowers your efforts to grow in this arena.

A Brief Introduction

By now you should have developed a feel for the three dimensions or movements. In subsequent chapters I will go into greater detail and deeper reflection, but for now a brief definition of each dimension will do. Let's start with Blue, or Heart.

Blue(Heart) is focused on the Other. Blue(Heart) is about OTHERness. Blue is concerned with what we *give to* the Other. It involves our interest in, listening to, and caring for the Other. A parent moves toward a child by nurturing and encouraging him or her. A lover moves toward the beloved with physical affection, erotic tenderness, or selfless giving. A supervisor moves toward her subordinates by listening to their needs and ideas and "catching them doing something right."[4] An employee moves toward his employer by putting his whole heart into a project. A society moves toward its people by caring for the less fortunate.

Blue(Heart) is also concerned with what we *need from* the Other. Dependency is tricky for most adults, but when it works, we get our genuine needs met. In families, a baby needs to be held and fed. A child may need to be helped with homework or guided through an emotionally difficult situation. A partner needs to be cared for and supported. In the workplace, an employee needs to be given guidance to feel equipped to do the job and to be listened to, and an employer needs to receive feedback and input on projects. In society, the poor and disadvantaged need help to get back on their feet in order to become self-sufficient and successful.

Whereas Blue(Heart) is concerned with the Other, the psychological orientation of Red(Power) is about Self. Red(Power) is about SELFness. This concern with self can either be a singular "I" or a plural "we." It could be about winning an argument with a friend (singular) or *my* football team defeating their opponent (plural). This movement has to do with competition, fight, prominence, and power. It has to do with exhibiting courage and candor even when others do not want to hear what we have to say.

There is a word that is commonly used in (cognitive-behavioral) psychology: *self-efficacy*. Self-efficacy is the belief in one's own competency or power, a belief that one is capable of performing in a way that attains a set of goals.[5] Others use the term *agency* to describe the same thing. When we say that someone has agency we are in essence saying that they have the means to get things accomplished. Red(Power)—self-efficacy and agency—has to do with how we control and manage our world.

In acting on the world for our own behalf, Red(Power) is about self-protection. Red(Power) is why we have fences, home security systems, and a standing army. We are moving against when we set a boundary with an intrusive friend or relative or when we have clear boundaries around time, such as running a meeting efficiently. When we hire a lawyer to represent us in a lawsuit, we hire a Lion to move against another and protect our needs.

Where Blue(Heart) is concerned about the Other and Red(Power) is fighting for Self, the psychological orientation of Yellow(Mind) is neither Self nor Other. Yellow(Mind) is about MINDfulness—fullness of mind. Yellow(Mind) is the capacity to step back and think about a situation rather than react to it. It is the capacity to *know* something about our self or the other without being entangled with either. It is the capacity to be calm in a storm and differentiated from provocations. It is the *scientific* function of society.

Another aspect of Yellow(Mind) involves *self-control*. It is the ability to endure and contain what we do feel. If I am angry about a situation, Yellow helps me "hold" those feelings—to think about them——rather than act them out. Yellow(Mind) is what makes us civilized (along with a little moving-toward). Without Yellow we would be mugging and maiming (Red) or mounting and merging (Blue) with everything and everyone we encountered.

Each of the movements can be positive or negative. For example, a positive Red would involve healthy competitiveness and candor; an unhealthy Red would

involve prejudice and bullying. In Chapter 1 we talked about the three (negative) ways that we react. We
also have three (positive) ways that we respond. So in
essence there are three dimensions but six manifestations: three positive and three negative.

ENERGY	DIMENSION/MOVEMENT -->		
	Toward/Blue (Heart)	Against/Red (Power)	Toward/ Yellow (Mind)
Positive (Creative and Connecting)	Cooperative Caring/ Empathy	Courageous Assertive/ Protect	Conscious Nonreactive
Negative (Destructive and Disconnecting)	Dependent Compliant/ Weak	Domineering Contemptuous	Detached Aloof

Table 2.3. Positive and Negative Energies of the
Three Movements/Dimensions

The Relationship Circle

Everyone moves in all three dimensions. And if a
dimension of movement does not show up in a healthy
way, it will express itself somehow, in a negative way.
To better depict this, let's look at a visual representa-
tion of this dynamic called the *Relationship Circle*.

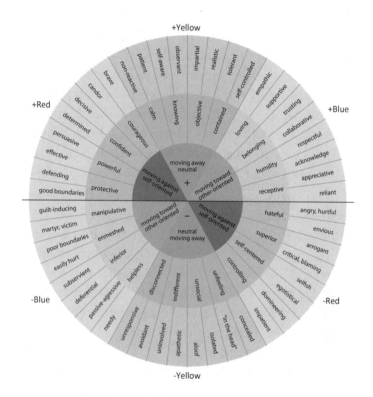

Figure 2.3. The Relationship Circle

The Relationship Circle is a graphic depiction of the three interpersonal movements or dimensions. The bottom half of the circle—or below the line—represents out-of-balance reactive behaviors (outer ring) and attitudes (middle ring) that arise from an imbalance in one or more of the core movements (inner circle). This imbalance results from insecurity, anxiety, and fear.

In his book *The Eight Habits of Love,* Ed Bacon—a frequent guest on Oprah Winfrey's *Soul* series—talks about the destructive aspects of negative emotions, especially fear, and the constructive power of love and its eight habits.[6] I greatly appreciate the distinction between destructive fear and life-giving love. When it comes to what motivates us, I believe that the opposite of love is not always hate but often *fear.*

In so many ways, hate is a manifestation of fear. *Homo sapiens* are often afraid and anxious; we are a very insecure species. Earlier in the chapter, I referred to a passage in the New Testament, where Paul of Tarsus endorses the three dimensions in the form of power, love, and a sound mind as the alternative, if not antidote to a "spirit of fear."[7] In his one simple exhortation, he identified the role of fear in human suffering. Nineteen centuries later, Freud would attribute most neurotic behaviors to anxiety, a form of fear, and would identify anxiety as our universal Achilles heel. The profound negative effects of fear (or anxiety) are found in the attitudes and behaviors below the line in the Relationship Circle.

Below-the-Line Attitudes and Behaviors

The bottom half of the circle is what some people would call "low" frequency energy. It is negative energy. It is "heavy" and burdensome. It is destructive. It leads to miscommunication rather than communication. Dynamically it causes regression rather than progression. In everyday language, it simply feels bad, and it makes things worse.

Wilfred Bion, one of the main contributors to the Interpersonal Triangle, was quick to suggest that his three ways of connecting or "linking" to others could either have a positive or a negative valence (energetic chemical charge). Current thought leaders[8] talk specifically about the nature of all living things being essentially energy and "vibrations." Many base this idea in part on recent scientific insights into the makeup of the universe at a sub-atomic level, which is believed to consist of nothing but (quanta of) energy.[9] Thus they conclude that all living things, including you and me, are essentially energy vibrating—positively or negatively.

The pain-body, our quantum packet of emotion-notions, exists below the line. Chapter 1 includes a quote by Eckhart Tolle, who defines the pain-body as a "negative energy field" that occupies your body and mind. Everything below the line is negative energy, and it feeds on pain.

Most negative human behavior can be found in one—or a blend—of these below-the-line behaviors and attitudes. These pain-body by-products throw us out of balance and make us relationally lopsided. In fact, these below-the-line reactions are by nature imbalanced.

Above-the-Line Attitudes and Behaviors

The top half of the Relationship Circle is higher-frequency energy, along the lines of what Brian Wilson from the Beach Boys would call "good vibrations." It fosters clear and compelling communication. It is light and flexible. It is free of pain-body and Ego. It connects with others. It corrects and affirms. It enhances positive outcomes and solves and resolves problems. It feels "good," and it makes things better.

The thought leaders who talk about energy underscore the importance of positive energy in optimal human interactions. And positive energy is more likely to beget more positive energy. In his book on emotional intelligence and leadership, Daniel Goleman emphasizes the observable dynamic of how a positive attitude or mood in a leader is contagious among all the people with whom he or she comes into contact.[10] As a result of this, morale shoots up and brings productivity with it.

I have seen this in my service work. I serve on a committee in California associated with the American Psychological Association called the Psychologically Healthy Workplace Awards. We identify and confer awards to organizations (big and small, for-profit and not-for-profit) that exemplify a psychologically healthy workplace. What we find over and over again is that these organizations are not only pleasant places to work, but they are profitable as well. It turns out that happy people are better employees: They get sick less, take off less time, stay in the job longer, and produce more. Positive energy yields positive results.

In his book *The Untethered Soul,* Michael Singer identifies a dynamic that is key to living fully and a hallmark of relating to the world above the line: openness![11] He suggests that if we can stay open to our experiences all the time, then energy will properly flow through our hearts, and we will live to our fullest. Below-the-line reacting closes us. It constricts and restricts our ability to move freely. It gets trapped and we get stuck. So whether we are holding onto a grudge, shutting off authentic emotions, or succumbing to the will of others, we obstruct the flow of positive energy. Above-the-line relating, on the other hand, opens our heart and keeps positive energy moving. So if we allow ourselves to be vulnerable and need others, forgive others and ourselves, are candid in our important relationships, and mindfully stay present in the moment, positive energy flows and moves through us.

St. Paul's reference to power, love, and a sound mind; Bacon's eight habits of love; Singer's openness and flow; and Tolle's transcendence over pain-body by conscious presence—they all flourish above the line, where human beings manifest their fullness, their *Dharma*. Dharma connotes the idea of fulfilling one's nature. And this is our highest nature: to live in dynamic balance and harmony above the line, unburdened, unstuck, and unencumbered. People refer to this state by any of a number of names. Some call it our Essential or True Self (who we are without pain-body), or god-Self (who we were "designed" to be). No matter what we call it, living energetically above the line is our Best Self. Has anyone ever reached this state on a consistent, enduring basis? I don't know. (Did Jesus or Buddha live above the line all the time?) All I know is that when I—on occasion—fire on all three cylinders, when I find my "sweet spot" and operate above the line for *any* amount of time, I am fully human and fully alive.

No Positive Movement Can Stand Alone

There is something notable about the top half of the Relationship Circle. It follows the principle of "one for all and all for one." If you start with a good, healthy Blue(Heart) and Yellow(Mind), but you are not able to do a healthy proactive Red(Power) (self-respect, healthy protection, and assertiveness), then you will soon be thrown out of balance and will tilt reactive −Blue and/or tilt reactive −Yellow.

Think of it as similar to a three-legged stool. If you cut one or two legs shorter, the stool top will not be level: It will be tilted. Or consider a tripod holding up a camera. If you lower a leg or two on a tripod, the camera on top will be lopsided and the picture you take (so to speak) will be lopsided. *There is no positive interpersonal movement unless all three are positive.*

You might say that there are times in life that require true Blue—acts of noble self-sacrifice—as is demanded of parents at times. Or perhaps there are times to call on pure Red in fierce but sanctioned competition, such as in sports. And ask any scientist: They aspire to unbiased Yellow objectivity. True! However, in these situations the other colors are avoided for a positive reason, not because of anxiety. On the other hand, if the self-sacrificing person is acting "selfless" because they are *afraid* to be Red, then we call it codependence, not love.

But there is more at play here than just balance. When all three modes are moving together, we not only get balance, but we get something a lot more interesting and dynamic. We get something transcendent. We get synergy—which we will soon discuss in Chapter 3.

Emotional Intelligence

Emotional intelligence (EI) is a newly coined term for a concept that we have known for a long time to be true. Emotional intelligence, simply stated, is the ability to recognize, understand, and effectively manage your emotions and behavior,[12] and the ability to recognize, understand, and effectively manage the emotions and behavior of others. Daniel Goleman popularized this idea in several books on the subject.[13] He has boiled the concept into four basic categories: self-awareness, self-management, social awareness, and relationship management.

	AWARENESS	BEHAVIOR
OTHER	Social Awareness	Relationship Management
SELF	Self-Awareness	Self-Management

Table 2.4. The Four Aspects of Emotional Intelligence

A good deal of research on EI has been done in the area of management and leadership. Although not all studies are unequivocal, the preponderance of research supports the idea that the higher the level of emotional intelligence, the more effective the leader; and, the lower the level of emotional intelligence, the poorer the leader's effectiveness. A boss who is overly demanding, impatient, and rude does not bring out the best out in people, but a boss who is firm and clear while being fair and positive will get us to reach our higher potential. No doubt the same is true in other relationships outside of work, such as with friendship, dating, marriage, parenting, and other important relationships. In essence, emotional intelligence is a measure of social and personal maturity. When we think of people who are mature, we think of people who, first and foremost, know themselves accurately and honestly. They have self-control; they know other people and know how to manage the relationships they are in without being manipulative brutes. In other words, these mature individuals are emotionally intelligent.

I hope that it is not difficult to convince you that the above-the-line behaviors and attitudes in the Relationship Circle that we just discussed are another way to describe and prescribe emotional intelligence. The descriptions of the mature person in the previous paragraph could just as easily describe the person living in the positive aspects of the three dimensions. Even a simple reflection corroborates this:

- Self-awareness is predominately Yellow(Mind) knowing or moving away,

- Self-management likewise is Yellow(Mind) self-control,

⚊ Social-awareness involves a great deal of Blue(Heart) empathy, and

⚊ Relationship management is Red moving-against influence, or agency.

	AWARENESS	BEHAVIOR
OTHER	Social Awareness +Blue(Heart)	Relationship Management +Red(Power)
SELF	Self-Awareness	Self-Management
	+Yellow(Mind)	

Table 2.5. Three Aspects of Emotional Intelligence

You might ask, "Why do we need another model; then?" First of all, any good tool chest has more than one tool. Sometimes we might want to grab Goleman's EI "square" to help understand ourselves, but at other times we might need the Interpersonal Triangle or the Relationship Circle to guide us. A second and more important reason lies in the Interpersonal Triangle's utility. In Chapter 3, I present a very useful application called Working the Triangle, which can be used in just about any interpersonal challenge to steer us back into balance. But once again, I get ahead of myself.

Think of the Interpersonal Triangle as a map. It is not the destination; it is the guide. How can a two-dimensional model make a difference in my complex, three-dimensional life? In the same way a two-dimensional map can help you find your way to a three-dimensional destination. You need a rest from the city, so you decide to take a trip to Cooperstown in Upstate New York. You get out a map of New York State in order to locate Cooperstown, and there at the southern-most part of Glimmerglass Lake, you find it. Only a fool would think that because you found the destination on the map that you found the destination itself, but it would be almost as foolish to think that you could jump into a car in Manhattan and get to the real Cooperstown without some guidance. The map is not the destination; the map is the guide. It is only as good as it realistically and accurately represents "the real world" (and if you actually follow its direction).

As you learn how to positively and naturally move through the three dimensions of the interpersonal world, you will be more effective, happier, and positive in relating to yourself and others.[30] My audacious goal is to help make the world a better place, one person at a time (starting with myself), and in so doing I humbly submit my offering to you, the Interpersonal Triangle. It is a map, a guide to help you—as it continues to help me—transcend the more reactive self and move toward a higher level of maturity and wholeness.

If you have not done so yet, go to *www.power-heart-mindfulness.com* and take the *Interpersonal Triangle Inventory*, or ITI. You can use the results of this inventory to answer the following questions about yourself.

Reflections and Musings

1. Which language or terms do you most identify with (see Table 2)? Least identify with? Why?

   If you have not done so yet, using the code that came with the book, go to *www.power-heart-mindfulness.com* and take the *Interpersonal Triangle Inventory*—or ITI. You can use the results of this inventory to answer the following questions about yourself.

2. Your interpersonal challenge: Whom did you pick for your setting and context—your spouse, child, boss, employee, parent?

3. Your positive movements.

   ⌃ Which positive movement(s) is the strongest for you? In what ways does that fit (and in which ways does it not fit)?

   ⌃ Which positive movement(s) is the weakest movement for you? To the extent that fits, why do you think this is the most difficult movement for you to use with them?

4. Your negative movements.

   ⌃ Which negative movement(s) is the weakest movement for you? This suggests the way you are least likely to initially react to your challenging person. Does that fit (and in which ways does it not fit)?

   ⌃ Which negative movement(s) is the strongest for you? Is this the way you most likely react to them? And if so, how do you generally do it?

Chapter 3
Working the Triangle

"But then I should not have had my wonderful brains!" cried the Scarecrow. *"I might have passed my whole life in the farmer's cornfield."*

"And I should not have had my lovely heart," said the Tin Woodman. *"I might have stood and rusted in the forest till the end of the world."*

"And I should have lived a coward forever," declared the Lion, *"and no beast in all the forest would have had a good word to say to me."*

L. Frank Baum, *The Wonderful Wizard of Oz*

One simple principle about the three relational movements is that each of us moves in all three dimensions: Blue(Heart/Toward), Red(Power/Against), and Yellow(Mind/Away). Even though some might "prefer" one movement or dimension over another, it does not mean that the other dimensions are not dynamically present. In the same way that all objects in the physical world exist in three dimensions—height, depth, and width—so, too, each individual moves in all three dimensions of the relational world. The most submissive, kind-hearted Blue(Heart) person has the very human capacity for anger, if not rage, within them. If cornered, even a bunny rabbit will bite.

I learned this lesson the hard way. I had been practicing as a therapist for only a short time when I met Mille. She was a sweet, fragile woman, demure and hesitant in every way. Each week she would tell me stories—with slumped shoulders—of her brute of a husband who, according to her report, was controlling, critical, and selfish. I felt badly for her, suffering under the tyranny of this bully.

After several sessions, I decided to challenge her. I wanted to explore *her* role in this apparently "bad" relationship. She became quiet and quickly changed the subject. I made note of this and determined that she was not ready yet. Then she missed her next session. When I called to reschedule an appointment, we agreed on a time during the next week. She missed that session as well and didn't return my subsequent call. I need to mention here that I had let her balance build. Of course she would pay me, I thought. Her "bad" husband made a good living and she was such a nice person. Not only did I never hear back from her, she never paid her balance.

Clearly, when there was the whiff of a suggestion that she might need to give up her "victim role" and take responsibility for herself, this very Blue(Heart) woman ran for the hills, acting as a Yellow(Mind). And while running, she happened to "forget" to pay. Yes, this sweet Blue(Heart) woman gushed negative energy Red (albeit in a passive way) by refusing to pay for services faithfully rendered. She was clearly out of balance.

How do we get out of kilter? We get out of balance when we are situationally or interpersonally "challenged," and we are not able to fully, positively, and successfully use all three of the positive, above-the-line movements. *Relation Rule: If for reason of habit or immediate anxiety we avoid the positive expression of one dimension, we almost always express the negative versions of the other movements.*

Take John, for example. His boss calls him into the office. She is angry because they were late on the delivery of a project that he worked on along with several others, and the client got very upset. She accuses him of "dropping the ball." He is initially upset because he has felt all along that she has not taken leadership on the project. However, he freezes in his seat when she confronts him. If his mind could have engaged at the moment (Scarecrow), he would have known that he was afraid of saying anything, fearing that he might express something that he would later regret. In that moment, time stops; he is unsure of what he really thinks. He is confounded, so he emotionally detaches (tilts Yellow) and apologizes for a crime he does not think he committed (tilts Blue). He feels "bad" rather than "mad." Because of his inability to go +Red at that moment, he is thrown out of balance, overdoing both –Yellow and –Blue.[1]

Elias Porter had a wonderful notion. He said that our weaknesses are nothing more than overdone strengths![2] When John was unable to express +Red appropriately, he over-expressed –Blue and –Yellow. He *reacted* from the bottom half of the Relationship Circle. And because of the low-frequency negative energy that comes from getting stuck (low flow), his response is ineffective if not hurtful—in this case to himself.

Betty had a very frustrating day at work. She lost a big client. Knowing this, her husband prepared a nice meal for her. When she arrived home, she found a lovely table full of her favorite foods. Looking over the thoughtful spread, she immediately noticed her mother's best serving utensils, which were not to be used except on special occasions. Without hesitation, she laid into her husband with a barrage of criticism, accusing him of being passive aggressive, thoughtless, and insensitive. "How many times do I have to tell you not to use my mother's utensils unless it is an important event?" What she could not tell him, however, was how upset she was that she had lost an account that day. Because she could not do +Blue, she overdid

–Red. It was low frequency –Red. It was pain-bodied –Red. Her reaction was demeaning, hostile, and destructive. She did not communicate what she really and truly felt. Her husband was trying to make her feel good with a special meal, but instead he was now set back on his heels defending himself.

Miguel was a major stakeholder in a mid-size business that he had started from scratch many years before. He was a very bright and gregarious person, perhaps too gregarious. He often found himself overly involved in everyone's affairs at work and kept poor boundaries, even with support staff, who looked up to him as the owner and boss. When events did not go Miguel's way, he would throw temper tantrums and explode with rage. What we discovered early in our coaching sessions was that he had difficulty with the Yellow(Mind) dimension. He was afraid that if he *moved away* (to use Horney's terminology) or stood back to consider, he would become marginalized, unimportant, and ineffective. His fears were aroused every time he thought he might be excluded. Because his Yellow(Mind) was underdeveloped, he would easily get out of balance with reactive –Blue (poor boundaries) and reactive –Red (rage). As a result, none of the staff liked working for him, and none of his partners liked to work *with* him. They all avoided him—ironically, the very thing that he feared most!

All of these people are examples of how easily we can get out of balance. Unfortunately, it does not take much to fall into these reactive patterns. If, in any given moment, one is unable to express a healthy version of an interpersonal dimension, one's whole ability to respond is thrown off balance. As a result, a person typically will become stuck, negative, and reactive. On the other hand, when all three modes are moving together we not only get balance, we get something a lot more interesting and dynamic. We get something transcendent. We get synergy!

Synergy

Synergy[3] comes from the Greek word *synergos*, meaning "working together." It is defined as the integration of two or more, in this case three, agents so that their combined effect is actually greater than the sum of their individual effects. In other words, when the three positive movements work together in a coordinated fashion, the quality of each individual movement improves: Our caring is deeper, our courage is stronger, and our knowing is wiser. The overall quality of our interpersonal relationships reaches new and remarkable levels. Synergy produces positive energy. Synergy is the engine that makes the Interpersonal Triangle dynamic.

On the surface, the interpersonal movements seem at odds with each other. For example, Red(Power) (regard for oneself) seems contradictory to Blue(Heart) (regard for others). However, one important quality of synergy is that each movement actually corrects the others. When the movements work together, each keeps the others from going out of balance.

When synergy takes place:

⅄ **Red(Power)** cannot be too mean; it is regulated by Blue's regard for others and Yellow's self-control and objectivity.

⅄ **Blue(Heart)** is never too weak and helpless because Red will not give up personal agency and Yellow will see things clearly.

⅄ **Yellow(Mind)** will never be too relationally isolated, because Blue's concern for others and Red's self-regard will make Yellow(Mind) appropriately present with others.

A second quality of synergy is that each interpersonal movement interacts with the others in a way that *augments* their overall effect. When our +Blue, +Red, and +Yellow work together, each dimension's distinctive strength improves the others and helps us become more whole and dynamic. Even though these attributes can appear contradictory, when they work in concert the result is transcendent!

Think of *The Wonderful Wizard of Oz*. By the time Dorothy reaches the witch's castle, her three companions are starting to work more like a team. Tin Man is passionate to save Dorothy, Scarecrow calmly comes up with ways to get into the castle, and Cowardly Lion is starting to show some nerve. They are no longer the detached Scarecrow on a pole in a cornfield, the helpless Tin Man frozen in the forest, or the nasty Lion bullying defenseless sojourners along the road. When the positive aspect of each companion starts to work together, synergy occurs. Dorothy is ready to do one of the more difficult tasks of her journey: melting the witch.

Empirical Support

I discovered compelling support for synergy in, of all places, an organizational research study. Researchers Robert Kaplan and Robert Kaiser did an important study[4] attempting to answer the "less-filling, tastes-great" dispute in the study of leadership. They asked the long-debated question: "Which is better? The traditional outcome-oriented, authority-based leadership style that they called *Forceful* or the people-oriented, empowering leadership style that they labeled *Enabling*?" To address this question they went into organizations and asked people to evaluate the leaders in their company. They asked if "Leader-A" was:

⋏ Too forceful.

⋏ Not forceful enough.

⋏ Just forceful enough.

Then they asked if the same "Leader-A" was:

⋏ Too enabling.

⋏ Not enabling enough.

⋏ Just enabling enough.

After they crunched all the numbers (as researchers like to do) they came up with, not hundreds of possibilities, but instead a cluster of four distinct categories of leaders which they labeled:

1. Lopsided Forceful. These were leaders who were described as having too much Force and not enough Enabling.

2. Lopsided Enabling. These were leaders who were described as having too much Enabling and not enough Force.

3. Disengaged. These were leaders who were described as not having enough Force or Enabling.

4. Versatile. These were leaders who were described as having just the right amount of Force and Enabling and knowledge of when to use them.

You can probably see why I like this study so much. When they reduced the hundreds of possibilities, they came up with four general categories that just so happen to match the three negative (below-the-line) dimensions and one dynamic interaction (made up of the three positive above-the-line dimensions):

1. Lopsided Forceful, who was out of balance for having too much Force (and not enough Enabling), is our –Red.

2. Lopsided Enabling, who was tilted for having too much Enabling (and not enough Force), is our –Blue.

3. Disengaged, who were out of kilter for not having enough Force nor Enabling, is our –Yellow.

4. Versatile, who had just the right amount of Force (+ Red) and Enabling (+Blue) *and* knew (+Yellow) when to use them. Kaplan and Kaiser's versatile leaders have synergy!

One of the four types of leaders noted in their study was rated as more effective than the other three. Do you want to take a wild guess which one? Versatile (synergistic) leaders were rated significantly higher in overall effectiveness than any of the other three. Who would you rather work for (be married to, be parented by, be friends with, be counseled by, or trust to make our laws)? A forceful person without empathy? A wishy-washy pushover with no backbone? A detached avoidant? Or a dynamically engaged, fair-minded, caring yet candid individual?

Speaking of parenting, there are similar findings in studies from that field. The parenting styles supported by research literature include authoritarian parents (those with "my-way-or-the-highway" approaches involving high demands and little emotional engagement), permissive parents (overly engaged parents who demand little and avoid confrontation), disengaged parents (characterized by low demand *and* low engagement), and authoritative parents (those who establish firm guidelines but are also responsive and emotionally engaged with their children). Can you see the pattern? Authoritarian parents tend toward –Red. Permissive parents show –Blue characteristics. –Yellow would be the disengaged parents. And, yes—you guessed it—authoritative parents are those who are synergistically operating from their sweet spot.

The lesson is that the goal of healthy and effective relationships is to achieve synergy—the dynamic interaction of all three above-the-line dimensions: +Red, +Yellow, and +Blue. This is never truer then when we are otherwise tempted to tilt. So whether we are leading a difficult board meeting at work, working through a difference with our spouse, parenting an unruly child, treating a client in therapy, or negotiating a proposal in Congress we want to fire on all three cylinders of our relational self. We want to move smoothly in all three dimensions of the relational world. We want to interact smoothly and "flow" with positive energy to its fullest.

The Synergy Pyramid

As this pertains to the Interpersonal Triangle, picture a pyramid. Think of the increasing positive energy as the three integrate, rising up to the tip of the pyramid where all the energy is focused at one point. Specialists will tell you that the strongest geometric structure is a triangle/pyramid; the strongest point is its tip. People who relate to others at the tip of the pyramid are powerful, loving, and mindful all at once. At the tip we are at our sweet spot. At the tip we flow with positive energy. At the tip we are our most complete ourselves.

Working the Triangle

Okay, so how does one achieve this synergy? How does a person move from imbalance and reactivity to balance and response-ability? It is simple, but takes a lifetime to master. I call the process Working the Triangle. It is based on the following profound premise: *The key to successful relationships is not about what you are doing that is negative but what you are* not *doing that is positive.* It is less helpful to focus on your –Red impatience or your –Blue co-dependency or your –Yellow detachment, than to realize what you are *not* doing that is positive. The best way to explain this is by a few examples.

Working the Triangle: An Example

Remember Miguel from earlier in the chapter? Miguel was a partner in a firm that he helped start. When not tilted (by his pain-body), he was an amiable person and brilliant businessman. However, when he became lopsided, he was a Purple tidal wave of intrusion (–Blue) and rage (–Red). After doing a thorough assessment of the company, we assigned ourselves to a partner. I had the good fortune to work with Miguel as his executive coach. During one of our earlier meetings, I showed him the Interpersonal Triangle. Together we established that he would become too –Blue and certainly too –Red in many of his interactions. We explored how this negatively impacted his partners, his staff, and the entire work culture. While looking at the triangle, I asked him a simple yet important question: "What dimension are you not using?" The answer was obvious: "Yellow," he said. We spent the next few months in our coaching sessions—*not* trying to make him less angry or intrusive, but instead finding ways to build more +Yellow responses into his interpersonal repertoire. As he began doing this, an amazing thing happened: synergy. Let me illustrate.

Miguel was a "difficult person" during partners' meetings. Whenever they would get together, he would dominate the meetings. Mary would say something then Miguel would say something. Tom would say something then Miguel would say something. Paul

would say something then Miguel would say something and then Miguel would say something and then
Miguel would say something. What we found during
our interviews of the partners was that all of them understandably hated being in meetings with Miguel and
would essentially tune him out whenever he talked.
Over the years, the company developed a culture of
avoidance. Because of this culture, which was exacer-
bated by fear of stirring Miguel's wrath, the partners
would sit silently, waiting for him to finish. This left
Miguel unencumbered in the meeting, while at the
same time ignored, irrelevant, and paradoxically ineffective. The meetings were too long and notably fruit-
less—a remarkably costly thing for any organization.

When this came up in our coaching session, I challenged him to do something that was unnatural for
him. I suggested that every time he wanted to speak
in a partners' meeting, he should instead make a mark
on a piece of paper and remain quiet. After five marks,
he was permitted to say what was on his mind. This
proved to be most difficult for him at first. However,
because he was eager to change, he eventually was
able to do it. And when he did, a remarkable thing happened. When he practiced this +Yellow behavior, he
calmed down and began to actually listen (+Blue). His
partners noticed a difference in him, and they began to
ask him what he thought. When he told them candidly
what he thought (+Red), they listened and often used
what he suggested. The mood and morale of the partners' meeting changed remarkably. The meeting became significantly more productive while taking much
less time.

They all became less reactive: Miguel less dominant (–Red) and the partners less detached (–Yellow), and they all responded to each other in a collaborative way (+Blue).

Let's break down the steps that Miguel used to achieve synergy and change.

In order to Work the Triangle we need to A.C.T.:

A.C.T.: The Three Steps of Working the Triangle

1. **A**cknowledge that we are reacting (not responding). Acknowledging that we are lopsided, tilted, or otherwise out of kilter is perhaps the most difficult aspect of Working the Triangle. Our Ego will often not allow us to see that we are having a problem (if not the problem itself). So we blindly react, thinking that we are responding reasonably. The Ego tells us that it is only the other's issue, never noticing that we are lopsided. Our pain-body does not have any other way to behave. It takes great courage (+Red) and humility (+Blue) to acknowledge (+Yellow) when we go lopsided. It took Miguel several coaching sessions to help him realize this.

2. **C**onsider or identify the dimension (or interpersonal movement) that you are not manifesting. This is the key to Working the Triangle. You must identify what dimension of the relational behaviors you lack. And here is why we

call it "Working the Triangle." You imagine the triangle and acknowledge what negative behaviors you are expressing. Using that information, it was easy for Miguel to identify his "missing movement." He was reacting with plenty of –Red and –Blue, but was missing healthy +Yellow.

3. **Try** positive behaviors from the missing color movement. Miguel felt unnatural practicing Yellow(Mind) behaviors, especially when he was stressed. He felt he was giving up, unimportant, and marginalized. His greatest fear since childhood, that he would be unimportant and ineffective like his father, was still driving him. It took a great amount of courage for him to do +Yellow behaviors at first, until he realized that when he did move away, he acquired new power that he never thought he had. *There is power in practicing the movement we fear or avoid.* It went further than that, however. He experienced synergy, and in so doing, was not only able to become more calm, mindful, and self-controlled (+Yellow), but his Blue(Heart) and Red(Power) behaviors moved up into the *positive* (above-the-line) realm. He actually listened to others (+Blue) and was able to tell his truth candidly (+Red), without becoming negative. He moved from reactive to response-able. He learned to Work the Triangle.

Confounded

A word about the missing movement is in order. When we have difficulty freely expressing a particular movement, we are often confounded. Confounded, by definition, means to be puzzled or confused. It means to mix up something with something else so that the individual elements become hard to distinguish. And that is exactly what happens when we get confounded in a particularly dimension. Betty was confounded around Blue(Heart). She mixed up energetic (healthy vulnerability) +Blue with reactive (weak dependency) Blue. And because of this she over reacted in –Red. Miguel, on the other hand, was confounded around Yellow(Mind). He could not distinguish a healthy (above the line) +Yellow from an unhealthy (below-the-line) –Yellow. He seemed to think that all Yellow was negative. And as a result of this he reacted in –Purple.

Groups

Working the Triangle can be used by any of us, anytime we go lopsided. In the examples above, we have considered individuals at home and at work, but this tool is not limited to individuals. It can be applied to groups of people as well: Teams at work, organizations of all types, sports teams, political parties, and even countries can practice Working the Triangle.

I worked with a large nonprofit organization whose mission was to feed and house the homeless in the community. They were about to undergo a significant restructuring and wanted to be ready for the changes, so they asked me to facilitate a daylong, off-site retreat to help them prepare for this major transition. As part of that day, I gave everyone the ITI (*Interpersonal Triangle Inventory*). We plotted everyone's scores to discover that the highest negative score for seven out of eight team members was in the Blue(Heart) dimension. Only the team leader had a different high (negative) score.

What did that mean? It meant that most of the people in the team were overly compliant, yielding, and appeasing. They had a culture of compliance. When seeing these results, I asked, "How do you make decisions as a team?" Their answer was notable. "We don't make decisions. Harvey tells us what he wants, and we do it." I then asked Harvey how he liked that arrangement. "I hate it" was his reply. "I pine for input and challenge."

In this case it was not an individual who was out of balance; it was a team that leaned lopsided Blue. How would they Work the Triangle? They would do it the same way. They had to (and did) acknowledge that they were lopsided—overly –Blue. They were also too –Yellow. They would become detached, passive, and ultimately, disconnected. They were a Green team. So what was missing? Red(Power).

They were confounded about Red(Power). Instinctively, they saw it as always and only bad, harmful and—God forbid—"uncooperative." I challenged them in the meeting to come up with a +Red solution. And so they did. They came up with a process they called CDQ-U, which stood for Challenge, Debate, and Question, then Unite. They agreed to build the

CDQ-U process into their weekly staff meetings by asking "hard" questions (Why? When? How?). They would challenge any new idea and debate alternatives. After doing this and coming up with a vetted outcome, *then* they would do what they did naturally: Get behind the idea and support it (+Blue).

Applications Past, Present, and Future

The most vital application of Working the Triangle is in the *present*. That is, when we become reactive and need to get back into balance. If we can catch ourselves going lopsided and then Work the Triangle in that moment, then we are way ahead of the game.

Working the Triangle in the present, however, is the most difficult to do. We often do not catch ourselves before we become reactive. When we discussed the limbic system in Chapter 1, we noted that this part of the brain is reactive by nature. It is automatic and intense. So in the heat of the moment, we are often past the point of no return. Our brain is aroused, our adrenaline is flowing, our muscles are tense, our perception is restricted, and our automatic thoughts impulsively go into fight–flight–freeze responses. It never occurs to us to stop and Work the Triangle, so we don't. The limbic system—with all its emotional memories, habits, presumptions, and fears—takes control of the cortex and begins to drive the cortical-car itself. Except for the most mature and mindful person, we are often "too far gone" to Work the Triangle amid the storm.

We have to wait for it to settle——minutes, hours, days, months, years, sometimes decades later.

In situations like these, what we have left is in the past and the future. Although it might be too late to respond in the present, it is never too late to learn from the past or plan tactically for the future.

The person, organization, or government that can learn from the past is the one better prepared for the future. We can always Work the Triangle in retrospect. When Working the Triangle in terms of past experience, you get to try on the missing movement in your imagination. We have known for a long time that we can learn new behaviors through our imagination. Clearly the most practical application of Working the Triangle is in the future. The present application of Working the Triangle is often too difficult to do, and the past is too late to have an effect. However, you can always use the Interpersonal Triangle to prepare you for future encounters.

Several years ago, I had the opportunity to work with a company that was too big for me to manage alone, so I invited a seasoned consultant to join me in the project. Helen was a powerful woman: opinionated, self-assured, and always in control. I am generally confident when working with colleagues, but when I interacted with her, I often became something of a "little boy" around her. For example, I would come into a planning meeting with my own ideas, but leave with only her ideas. After many months on the project, we reached a critical impasse in our working relationship, and I had to say something. I did not want to react to her as I would typically react, so I intentionally Worked the Triangle in preparation for the meeting. I was well aware of my −Blue reaction: overly adapting to her point of view. I also knew that I would easily become detached, passive, and withdrawn—a −Yellow reaction. What did I have to integrate? What attitude and behaviors did I have to try on with her? Red(Power), of course! So I determined beforehand what I wanted to say to her, organized my talking points, and committed myself—no matter how uncomfortable and unnatural it might feel—to sticking to my talking points. I Worked the Triangle—ahead of time.

An interesting thing happened when I went into the meeting with Helen. I was very anxious. I remember my voice shaking when I started. But I was committed to trying on +Red candor with her. I told her what I saw and what I wanted. Every time she told me something different, I respectfully returned to my talking points. I do not know if she was in a Blue mood that day or if the ensuing synergy that I was enjoying dynamically changed our interaction, but we ended up engaged in a very constructive conversation. I left with my mind intact, and we had a common understanding of what each of us needed.

I often use the past and future applications of Working the Triangle when I work with the executives that I coach. First we debrief important encounters that they may have had since our last coaching session using the Interpersonal Triangle. If they reacted in a lopsided way, we identify the movement(s) that they did not use. We explore why they did not use it, identify the relevant emotion–notion confounding that movement, and debate its legitimacy. From there we imagine how it might have been different had they incorporated the positive expression of the missing movement. Then we consider future encounters with the same person or similar situations. We think about how they typically react to this person or situation, and we commit to trying on more of the missing movement that we have identified. You can see now how I did this with Miguel. I asked him to try on Yellow(Mind) behaviors by stepping back intentionally in partner meetings.

I also did this with a client named Debbie, who had just been promoted. She had been asked to lead a new division in the company, which concurrently earned her the right to be part of the executive team. She was the first female to join it. During the meeting she found herself shrinking, automatically deferring to the men in the group, just as I had with Helen. Even when they asked her opinion, she drew a blank. Her reaction was –Yellow. In our coaching session that followed, we talked about what kept her from both Blue(Heart) and especially Red(Power) attitudes and behaviors. We discussed her long-established narrative—her emotion–notions that dictated how she saw herself in reference to other people, especially men in authority. We then considered how she could try on some good Blue and Red behaviors in the next executive team meeting.

The combination of +Red and +Blue behaviors yields +Purple "engagement" behaviors. It was these social and leadership engagement behaviors that she needed to incorporate to establish herself as a company leader and a dynamic executive team member. Over the next few months of coaching, we reviewed past episodes and prepared for future encounters where she could practice +Purple engagement. She learned these behaviors so well that in response to her newfound +Red, the company owner was concerned that she was no longer happy since she was no longer passive. He became afraid that she might leave and was relieved to find out that, quite the contrary, for the first time she was actually enjoying her work.

How to Use the Rest of This Book

In the next three chapters, I am going to cover each interpersonal movement or dimension in detail. For those of you who are curious and have the time, I invite you to join me in taking a deep dive, exploring the three dimensions of what makes us human. However, if nothing else, read the chapters that are relevant to the interpersonal movements that most affect you. You can know this in one of a few ways:

➚ If you have not done so already, take the ITI. From your scores you can determine which interpersonal movement affects you most and which chapter you need to read and apply to yourself.

➚ You might be facing a "difficult" situation now, and you already know how you are reacting. By Working the Triangle you can identify the interpersonal movement that you need to "try on." For example, if you find yourself constantly giving in to your child (reactive Blue), you might want to explore the related sections in the Blue chapter regarding "ontological fears" and then read the chapter on Red(Power) to learn how to set better boundaries with your child.

➤ There is someone—a spouse, a child, a boss—who is a "difficult person" in your life. You might want to read certain sections of the relevant chapter. For example, if your spouse is reactive –Red, you might want to review the fears and anxiety section of the Red chapter to get insights into which fears are really driving that.

Reflections and Musings

Following are some additional questions that can help you integrate and understand the material in this chapter by reflecting on circumstances in your own life. Pick a relationship that is challenging to you now (it could be someone that you are dating, your spouse, a child, a boss, or an employee) and reflect on the questions:

1. How do you tend to react to this person when you are challenged or disagree?

   Do you become angry and defensive (Red)?

   Do you give in and adjust to their opinion (Blue)?

   Do you detach emotionally and try to avoid the conflict (Yellow)?

   Some blend of the above?

2. In light of your response above, which positive movement or dimension is missing in your reactions?

The ability to tell your truth, assert your needs, and set boundaries (+Red)?

The ability to empathize with the other person's concerns and needs (+Blue)?

The ability to objectively look at the situation and know each person's part (+Yellow)?

3. Which of the missing movements do you want to "try on" next time there is an impasse with this person, and how?

+Red

+Blue

+Yellow

It's important to understand that the Interpersonal Triad model is less a description of our personality and more a depiction of how we act and react relationally in any given situation. By now—if you've read any of the first three chapters—you should have a fairly good idea of your relational predispositions and the tendencies of others in your life as well.

Here's something to help you lay the groundwork:

1. In my role with (spouse, child, boss, etc.)

I tend to react in (circle): –Blue –Green –Yellow –Orange –Red –Purple

2. In my other role with (spouse, child, boss, etc.)

I tend to react in (circle): –Blue –Green –Yellow –Orange –Red –Purple

3. Based on what I selected above (Check all that apply)

   If I tend to react in –Blue I should consider reading more about Yellow and/or Red.

   If I tend to react in –Green I should consider reading more about Red.

   If I tend to react in –Yellow I should consider reading more about Blue and/or Red.

   If I tend to react in –Orange I should consider reading more about Blue.

   If I tend to react in –Red I should consider reading more about Yellow and/or Blue.

   If I tend to react in –Purple I should consider reading more about Yellow.

Chapter 4

Moving Against and the Power Dimension

I am Self. I am King; I am Queen. I rule. I know what I want and I get it. If there is a choice between either you or me, I pick me. I have agency—personal power. I am the strongest so I get to survive . . . perhaps thrive. Sometimes I exist in first person plural: "My family, my team, my religion, my ethnicity, my political party, my country. I diverge: My family—not yours, my team—not yours, my religion—not yours, my ethnicity—not yours, my political party—not yours, my country—tis of thee. I protect and preserve. I have a fence around my house and a standing army. I am courage; I do brave things. I am candor; I tell

the truth (my truth) whether you want to hear it or not. I say "no." The world is a dangerous place . . . I will survive."

Musings in the Key of Red

The psychological orientation of the Power dimension, Red, is about the Self. At the least, this "moving against" dimension (as Horney conceptualized it) is concerned with the Self's survival and, at most, its dominion over others and nature—with a certain level of interest in personal fulfillment and happiness somewhere in between these two concerns.

Red(Power) exists as "I"—first-person singular desires: I want to win; I want to be safe; I want my needs met; I want to save face; I want to be respected; I want to take care of myself; I want my bill passed in Congress. It is self-centered in the best sense of the word *and* in the worst sense of the word. In the best sense of the word it is about self-love, self-fulfillment, self-care, self-respect, and personal agency or power. It the worst sense of the word it is about self-centeredness, self-indulgence, and down-right shameless selfishness.

Red(Power) exists as "we," which embodies first-person plural desire: I want my team to win; I want the needs of my family to be met; I want our brand to be the best in the market; I want my neighborhood and my country to be safe. Everything that we might do that is Red individually can also be applied to our societal selves. We are hopelessly social creatures and therefore we do all three dimensions in identified groups—we think together as Yellow(Mind), we take care of others as a group as Blue(Heart), and we do things together as well as Red(Power). For example, we hunt together. We also compete and fight together against the outside threats that face us—real or imagined. For as long as history recalls, we have lived and survived in groups. And as long as we've lived in tribes we've fought together against others, whether as defenders or aggressors. This "we" expression of Red(Power) brings up an important dynamic common to all three dimensions.

Divergence, Convergence, and Observance

Each of the three dimensions relates to others in a distinct way. If you are in Red(Power) mode, you *diverge*; if you are Blue(Heart) you *converge*; and if you are moving in Yellow(Mind) you *observe*. We'll talk about converging and observing in subsequent chapters, but for now we'll focus on Red's tendency to diverge. Red(Power) is highly attuned to differences rather than similarities. "Did you see those two men kissing? How disgusting!" This same socially conservative person would probably not pay much attention to a heterosexual couple kissing. The Red(Power) dimension divides people into "me versus you" and "us versus them." I have little doubt that this is a by-product of evolution wherein the ability to mark differences would improve one's chances of survival. It was necessary for our ancestors to form identities around tribes who would survive by distinguishing themselves from other tribes.

This divergence can be positive. In a world where we all share more than 99 percent of the same DNA, it is nice to know that we have a little bit of individuality and distinctiveness. Carl Rogers, who is considered one of the founding fathers of humanistic psychology, popularized the term *self-actualization*. He defines self-actualization as the drive to fulfill one's unique potential and to achieve the highest level of "human-beingness."[1] He said that we all have a drive to both belong (Blue) and to self-actualize (Red), to become who we uniquely are among the billions of not-us others.

I am a partner in a firm that specializes in work with *corporate culture*.[2] To me, corporate culture is the personality of a group. If you walk into Google you will not have the same impressions as you would if you were to walk into IBM. They have different cultures—different personalities, if you will. And in this way Google and IBM diverge. They have many things that are the same, or converge (e.g., they both use computers), but they are also different and unique from each other. Being different is manifested in the Red(Power) dimension.

However, divergence taken too far can be very destructive. In its extreme form, divergence is the basis of unproductive, if not destructive, prejudice. We'd be tempted to think that this is unique to humans alone. But you need only take our little dog Mona for a walk. When she walks with her friend Terra, she is friendly and cooperative. However, if she encounters another dog en route—especially if it occurs in what she considers "her territory"—her teeth are bared and aggression is activated. So this xenophobia—fear of foreigners—is not unique to humans. The extreme manifestation of

Mona's –Red(Power) divergence might be a loud growl or at worst an attempted bite. On the other hand, our species has recorded such events as Hitler's holocaust, Stalin's murder of millions of his opponents within the Soviet Union, the Turks' attempted annihilation of Armenians, and—let's not forget—America's genocide of our own indigenous people and ongoing possession of slaves. In fact, human history is riddled with examples of the maligning and killing of those who are not like "us," whoever "we" may be.

However, this phenomenon does not take place only on a large, and thus catastrophic, scale. It happens every day to all of us in some way. We all have emotional reactions to someone who diverges from the mainstream—or "us." I consider myself a progressive man, but I still catch myself subtly reacting to someone who differs from me by virtue of skin color, nationality, religion, sexual orientation, or other characteristics. I am not proud of that, but I am subject to the hundreds of generations of conditioning that are imbedded in my inherited emotion–notions and implicit narratives. This conditioning is a by-product, no doubt, of evolution based on the fear of the unknown and perceived threats to our survival. And we are still afraid; to a frightening degree we are afraid.

So much human suffering—on both small and large scales—has come from this instinctive intolerance of difference and/or the exploitation of those who are not like us. When will we find a synergy that includes more +Green—Blue(Heart) inclusion and Yellow(Mind) objectivity—in how we address those who are different from us? Soon, I hope!

Power as Agency

The Power, or Red dimension, is wonderfully depicted in the great American myth, *The Wonderful Wizard of Oz*, in the character of the Lion. The Lion wanted to be King of the Forest. In other words, he wanted to rule in his own self-prescribed psychological territory or domain. Don't we all, at least to some extent? The answer is yes and maybe. There are some whose self-prescribed domain extends far past their own boundaries, overlapping many others. These are the controlling people of the world. At some time in your life, you likely worked for one of these dominant despots. Perhaps you had a controlling parent or a bossy child. You might have a domineering partner or spouse. (Or you might be a control freak yourself.) People like this feel the need to control everybody and everything that comes their way.

On the other hand, there are some people who have very little domain to speak of. They constantly and automatically yield to others. If they have an original thought or feel a personal need, it soon evaporates when they come in contact with someone else's needs or ideas. They live in self-doubt, waiting for someone else to verify "their" reality. We often call these people "co-dependent."

Some people may be dictators in one situation, for example at work—and are subservient in other situations—for example at home with a Red(Power) spouse or even willful children. I work with several executives who are in command of hundreds of people at work but as soon as they cross the threshold of their house they completely bend a knee to their spouse. And of course we mustn't neglect to mention those balanced Courageous Lions who have a realistic sense of their domain and take charge accordingly. They do not "need" to control others but they are not interested in losing their own autonomy either.

There is a wonderful word that depicts the essence of the "Lion" Power dimension: *agency*. I love this word. Typically, we use this word to describe a business or organization. But it has another use in the English language when describing a person. A person who has agency is a person who has power, the capacity to do something, strength, control and influence, political control and authority. A person with agency is a person who is skilled, competent, and has the necessary energy to affect his or her life as needed. Red(Power) is about this kind of agency or power. It is how we get our way, how we meet our needs, and how we protect ourselves. It is interpersonal in that it demonstrates power with others, but it is also ecological, demonstrating power over the world in which we live.

Genesis 1:28 says that "God blessed them and said to them, 'Be fruitful and increase in number; fill the earth and subdue it. Rule over the fish in the sea and the birds in the sky and over every living creature that moves on the ground.'"[3] This Old Testament God is directing us to have dominion, or stewardship, over the earth. This is one time we actually obeyed. In just a few short millennia, *Homo sapiens* have taken charge in a huge way. It was only yesterday that we hunted and gathered in small tribes with simple tools and crude weapons. Now we have super-computers and massive weapons. As I mentioned, at the time of this writing I am traveling to the East Coast to facilitate a workshop. To get there, I am flying (in the sky) in a large metal object they call a jet. I am going to be able to cross a span of three thousand miles in a few hours rather than a few months. I am typing on this thing on my lap called a computer, which can process information at lightning-fast speeds. Less than two centuries ago I would have had to write this out with a simple pen on coarse paper and there would only be one copy (unless I was moved to scribble it out all over again). And— oh yes—I'm running this computer thing on electricity stored in a small object called a battery. Need I say more? We obeyed God; we have dominated the Earth. Good job, everyone!

With our Red(Power) ambitions and drive we have cured diseases; we have built roads and vehicles to drive on them. We have curtailed in small ways some of Mother Nature's assaults by building strong edifices and predicting weather, although my personal feeling, since I live in California, is that we still have some work to do regarding earthquakes. Nevertheless, we've built incredible repositories of knowledge about the universe we live in.

However, as I have said repeatedly in this book, there is always another side. I ate a vegetarian meal on today's flight, but if I had ordered chicken or beef I would have indirectly subjected another living creature to unnecessary horror. The chicken would, in all likelihood, have been given vaccines and antibiotics to make it more productive while being permanently confined to a crowded shed, unable to run free. It would have been no better for the cow that would have provided me with beef. It would have been injected with larger doses of antibiotics, a hormone-filled pellet would have been implanted under the skin in the animal's ear, and it would have been kept in a crowded feedlot with minimal exercise in order to increase its fat and make it tastier. I am not arguing for a vegan lifestyle (we'll discuss this later in this chapter). I only want to show that we sometimes dominate the environment too much—without the mindful respect and care for the earth and its fellow sojourners that would come with a more +Yellow and +Blue approach. In contrast, consider how our Native American brothers hunted. They blessed and prayed for the game that they were about to kill, knowing that their need to eat should not justify a thoughtless disrespect for life.

The need for +Yellow and +Blue goes beyond our treatment of animal life, of course. We mindlessly pollute our environment, for sort-sighted gains and convenience. And now we find ourselves on the precipice of self-engineered disaster as the environment spits back at us in the form of global warming and disease-causing pollutants. (We also mindlessly pollute our bodies with unnatural additives, hydrogenated fats, excessive cornstarch, inordinate amounts of processed foods, and slow-acting poisons like refined sugar.)

But there is no misuse of power worse than the sort we exercise over each other in small—and not-so-small—ways every day. Most of us remember the

Great Recession of 2008, brought about in large part by the short-sighted greed of a few bankers, along with a majority of politicians, who did not have the wisdom of Yellow(Mind), the care of Blue(Heart) nor the courage of Red(Power) to govern for the good of everyone. The hardship that followed rippled through the entire country and the world. How many people lost jobs, homes, dignity, health—and for some, even life—because of the abuse of power by a few? This happens weekly on a large scale and in numerous ways (think of ISIS, police shootings, political corruption, etc.). But it also shows up every day in local ways as those with power prey on those who are more vulnerable. How many spouses psychologically, and at times physically, abuse their partners? How many adults abuse children—psychologically, physically, and even sexually? I write a blog for an organization called 1in6. They adopted their name from a statistic that is startling. One out of six adult males will have been sexually abused at some time during their childhood. It is twice as often for females. This is an abominable abuse of power.

Then there are the more subtle everyday abuses. The "little" power trips we all take that will never make the nightly news. Every time we thoughtlessly criticize one of our children or bully a spouse or an employee we are exhibiting –Red: the negative aspects of Red on the Relationship Circle.

It is easy to blame the individuals who are in control for these abuses of power. But the real problem goes beyond simply the individuals who happen to be in command at the time. Most of us would succumb if we were in the same positions of power. It takes a man or woman of immense integrity to wield great power without abusing it. The deeper problem has to do with us as a species. We are insecure; we are unconscious; we are out of balance. We do not know how to be in harmony with ourselves first, and to carry that on to our relationships with one another and our world. We do not know how to balance power with mindfulness and heart.

The Place of Red in Society
Competition

Those who believe in a personal Creator sometimes wonder why God would have designed a world filled with carnivores. Think about it. Why create a world where it is natural for creatures to kill and eat each other? The very fact that we cannot live without something else dying is a sobering reality. Whether there is a Being who made it this way or it's the by-product of the whims of evolution (or both) we cannot get around the fact that the Red(Power) approach is part of living on this planet. Maybe there is a planet somewhere that has no Red(Power), just Yellow(Mind) and Blue(Heart). But what would this two-dimensional world look like?

Every so often someone comes along with an idea that changes the way we think. Consider people like Buddha, Jesus, Mohammed, Galileo, Freud, and Einstein. Charles Darwin was such a man. His *The Origin of Species* categorically changed how we look at life on this planet. In this breakthrough work,

Darwin described what he called natural selection. It was Herbert Spenser who, after reading the works of Darwin, coined the phrase "survival of the fittest," which even Darwin used in his later works. It is now believed that differential reproduction, rather than "survival of the fittest," is the mechanism of natural selection but the idea itself did survive and is a key driver in the Red(Power) dimension. Red is the dimension of our drive to survive and to be strong, if not the strongest. Eat or be eaten. Many of us do not like this truth, but it is our reality all the same. I believe, of course, that we can transcend this reality by the integration of Blue(Heart) and Yellow(Mind)—but I get ahead of myself.

Survival of the fittest is a concept that lays the framework for what is clearly one of the main dynamics of Red(Power) in society: competition. *Merriam-Webster's Collegiate Dictionary* defines competition as "the act or process of trying to get or win something (such as a prize or a higher level of success) that someone else is also trying to get or win." Whether engaged in by an individual (such as in a singles tennis match or trying to win an argument) or by a group (such as a soccer team vying for the World Cup or a corporation's bid to gain market share), there is something that is inherently competitive within human beings.

We see the reality of Red-driven competition throughout society. Early in a family's life, we have our children playing on sports teams—against one another. They compete on a karate mat or during a spelling bee. Even toddlers will compete over a toy. Teachers hand out "student of the month" awards—to the same kid each month. We are hopelessly competitive. Even when we try to make something noncompetitive it does not seem to work. Just ask any child on a T-ball team who is winning (or losing) and he can tell you—even though they're not supposed to be keeping score. We compete to get the best grades in order to get into the best colleges. We compete in college to get the best jobs, and once in those jobs we compete to get the best promotions. Whether we like it or not, we are competitive. And whether we like it or not, competition makes us better at whatever we do.

Competition pushes us to run faster, think clearer, and work harder. In so many ways competition has made us better as a species and as individuals. People who are averse to –Red(Power) behaviors and attitudes often are also afraid of competition. The most obvious fear associated with competing would be the fear of losing. But sometimes it is actually a fear of winning. A person could certainly feel "bad" for "beating" someone else. This type of fear is common among people with disproportionately prominent Blue(Heart) and, of course, underdeveloped Red(Power)..

One of the most important ways of understanding Red's competitiveness as it pertains to society is to understand the free enterprise system. Our economic system is based on capitalism. Capitalism is based on competition. And competition is driven squarely in the Red dimension. Capitalism and the free enterprise system inherently and implicitly leverage competition to drive both superior products and services while at the same time trying to keep prices "competitive," as they say.

There *have* been attempts in our recent history to create economic systems based primarily on Blue(Heart) ideals. Communism would be one such experiment that, as we know, ultimately and unequivocally failed. Human beings don't quite seem able to share perfectly equally no matter how ideological we are about that idea. Some people just want to have the biggest piece of the control and power pie, which is a clear manifestation of Red(Power). So in essence, the free enterprise system leverages our innate tendency to compete and win. Please note, however, that we are not able to engage in this without government regulations. Why? Because we cheat. Speaking of cheating, let's talk about morality as it relates to Red(Power).

Red Morality

Many are tempted to think that Red is without morality. After all, Red's focus is on the self and not the other. Think again. As in all three dimensions, there are morals and deep-seated values that emerge, even from the Red(Power) dimension. I will identify four.

Courage

Any child between the ages of five and 95 can name the attribute sought by the Lion in *The Wonderful Wizard of Oz*. It was courage! And just as we have a vast record of "bad people" doing bad things to each other throughout history, we also have a record—albeit perhaps smaller—of people acting with great courage, even to the point of self-sacrifice. And one thing about courage is that whenever we see it, we are both impressed and inspired.

It is important to remember that courage is not the absence of fear. In fact, if there is no fear then there isn't any real courage, either, only habit or madness. Courage is present when we act in spite of fear, whether because we are responding to firm core beliefs or perhaps because of a human need that is compelling. Sometimes we act courageously for our own benefit. We may need to say something difficult to our spouse, or perhaps an employee. Sometimes we have to push through a difficult task despite the temptation to give up. At other times, courage is a selfless act. For instance, we may be moved to donate a kidney to a loved one. Either way, courage helps us do important things that we would not otherwise do.

Candor

One of the most important manifestations of courage occurs in the form of candor. Candor is the quality of being open, sincere, direct, and honest. Presumably for most people, this happens in small ways every day, in our community interactions as well as in the home. One thing that I have noticed consistently when I work with executives who are strong in their +Red is their ability to tell the truth as they see it without undue fear of the listener's reaction. Whether they are talking to an employee, a peer, or even to someone up-line, they are honest and direct. I find this refreshing.

I often say that if you really want to know the truth, ask someone with a healthy dose of Red(Power). What happens if you ask someone who is predominantly Blue(Heart)? They will generally tell you what they think you want to hear. A Red(Power) is not under such a compulsion. Ask a Blue(Heart) person if your dress makes you look fat, and they will probably tell you that you look great. If you ask a Red(Power) the same question, you'd better be ready for the truth, whatever that may be.

This Red(Power) attribute of candor is profoundly important to society. Civilization needs its prophets in order to stay civilized. Without our truth-tellers, society would at best stagnate and at worst become insufferable. Just think of regimes where the person in control prohibits free speech. What they are prohibiting is the benefit of people giving divergent opinions—telling their truth. Think of those known for outspoken truth like Jesus, Martin Luther King, Jr., or Gandhi. They spoke truth with unapologetic authority and, like many others, lost their lives as a result.

Red attributes can be observed on a group level as well. I've marched for peace along with thousands against the war in Vietnam—a confession that certainly dates me. History presents us with others who have "protested" to right-entrenched injustices: for instance, to overthrow the heavy-handed rule of the British Empire in the American Colonies, to deconstruct the institution of slavery, to secure the right of women to vote, eventually expanding the fight for equal rights under the law for everyone. Society needs people who will tell the truth—even if we do not want to hear it—in order for us to grow and change.

One of the most important things that I do as a therapist and consultant is to tell the truth. We all have blind spots. In all likelihood, your marital problems are not entirely due to your spouse alone. If you think so, you likely have a blind spot to your contribution to the problem. As a therapist, it is my responsibility to help my clients see the whole truth, which requires me to tell them what I see even if it will be difficult for them to hear. I have the same duty when I work with business leaders. Executives are notorious for not wanting to hear bad news, especially if their behavior is the bad news. In a careful way, it is my responsibility to tell them that the "Emperor does not have clothes."

Ambition

People who function well in the Red(Power) zone are often ambitious. They get things done; they make things happen. They aim high and they don't give up. Think Thomas Edison. The man never gave up. He kept trying and trying until he got it. And because of this, you can read this paragraph at night without straining your eyes in candlelight.

Ambition is sometimes seen as a bad word. However, in and of itself ambition is not bad. It *becomes* "bad" (destructive, negative, harmful) when it is not corrected by healthy +Blue and +Yellow. Without the corrective balance of +Blue and/or +Yellow, a person's ambition is often realized at someone else's expense. It is this brand of ambition that goes beyond fair competition and instead becomes ruthless. An extreme example of this type of ambition can be seen in the character Francis Underwood from the TV series *House of Cards*, masterfully played by Kevin Spacey. There was little Underwood would not do to get what he wanted, even to the point of murder. I have no tolerance for ruthlessly ambitious people, but I have great respect for people who have a healthy ambition that drives them to be and do all that they can.

Self-Protection

I write this third positive attribute of Red(Power) for all the co-dependents reading this book. It is for all the people who cannot say no when it is in their best interest to do so. I write this for everyone who stays on the phone too long with their out-of-touch, self-absorbed mother who would take time away from your responsibilities to other loved ones, complaining about her aches and pains and gossiping about people you don't even know. I write this for the woman who goes out on a third date when the first two dates were awful. I write this for all of those people—whether men or women—who are afraid to ask their spouse not to criticize them in public.

The ability to protect oneself is not only a necessity for survival it is a responsibility. Who else is going to take care of us if we don't? And when people take on the responsibility to protect themselves when it is within their power to do it, they are exhibiting healthy +Red.

Red Reactions

In Chapter 1 we discussed the notable problem of human reactivity. Our proclivity toward reactivity is the instigator of numerous forms of suffering. It was in Chapter 1 that we introduced Eckhart Tolle's idea of "pain-body." If you remember, pain-body is the accumulated, un-integrated, and coagulated pain that we've experienced earlier in our life that was never dealt with (metabolized) and which we can readily re-experience as painful emotion when triggered. It is the part of our psyche (mind, soul) that gets inflamed when we are reactive, often in concert with our Ego being offended. Our Ego is the part of the mind that is mindlessly bent on defending its sense of importance, often at the expense of others, reality, and its hosts: you and me.

There are numerous ways we can react in −Red, underscored by our emotion−notions and driven by a pain-body reactivation and threatened Ego. For some ideas on how we can react in −Red refer to the below-the-line Red in the Relationship Circle (in Chapter 2). Here are just a few to note.

Hate

Hate is anger without the corrective mediation of +Blue and +Yellow. Hate intends to hurt rather than be hurt. It seeks revenge. It takes no prisoners. It has no guilt to own, but only offense to be taken. The inflamed pain-body corresponds (literally co-responds or reacts) with the Ego. They are a tag team, if not versions of the same psychological "thing." A pain-body inflamed in the color −Red is mean, angry, and . . .

Blaming

Homo sapiens like to blame. One of the characteristic Ego moves of the –Red dimension is to blame. When we are in a reactive pain-bodied state, all of us at some time (and for some of us all the time) attribute the problem to someone or something else. This is a characteristic –Red solution. The psychological process of blaming is based on what we call projection. Projection is the misattribution of one's undesired thoughts, feelings, or impulses onto another person. In Chapter 1, I talk about the necessity of "shameless ownership of our side of the equation" in order for us to grow and mature. This would be the opposite of blaming, and it is necessary for anyone who intends to grow and mature.

Resentment

I think of resentment as fermented anger. Anger is an emotion that is biologically necessary. Anger is meant to be a temporary feeling to be used at the moment and then moved through. That's why they call it *emotion*: it moves. However, when we hold onto anger (or its more intense cousin, hate) it ferments and becomes, as one dictionary has it, an imbedded "indignant displeasure or persistent ill-will at something regarded as a wrong, insult, or injury."[4] There is an obsessive aspect to resentment. You just can't stop thinking about the perceived injury weeks, months, years—even decades—later. The important thing to understand about resentment is that it is corrosive to the soul. It eats away at people. I believe that it can even make people sick unto death.

Envy

Many people are plagued with envy (for what others have) and jealousy (for *who* they have). They cannot be at peace—let alone grateful—for what they have because Michael still has a better job, Kim gets to travel more, Nancy eats anything she wants and is still thinner. There is a verse in the Bible that says, "Rejoice with those who rejoice and mourn with those who mourn."[5] Doing this connects us, which is beneficial to our physical and mental health in a number of ways. Envy does the opposite: It mourns with those who rejoice and rejoices with those who mourn, which leads to disconnection. This makes envy one of the most destructive human emotional states, because it engenders hate for the person or group that is envied. Some of the most violent human deeds have grown from envy, including murder, genocide, and war. The opposite of envy is gratitude. People who do not entertain envy instead express gratitude for who they are and for all the good things that they have—and researchers confirm that such people gain a great deal in both health and happiness as a result.

Narcissism

Entire books have been written about narcissism. It is enough to say here that narcissism is a fusion of unhealthy –Red and the Ego. Narcissists have an inflated sense of their own importance, a deep-seated need for admiration, and a lack of empathy for others. There are two dirty little secrets you need to know about narcissists. One is that narcissists are immature.

It is normal for a 4-year-old to be self-centered; it is not for a 44-year-old. Something occurs in the narcissist's life to arrest their development. The second dirty little secret is that narcissists are deeply insecure. They actually have a fragile sense of self that is vulnerable to the slightest criticism. They just hide this insecurity inside a gigantic Ego. Mature people feel good enough about themselves that they do not have to be preoccupied with themselves. Their self-esteem is intact enough that they have room to empathize (+Blue) and can take criticism in stride (+Yellow).

There is, of course, much more that could be said about reactions that occur in the color theme of −Red, but let's move on to managing these reactions.

What if You Are a −Red Reactor?

What if you have a tendency to react in −Red when you are provoked or engaged with your pain-body? What if you find yourself too often behaving in the −Red portion of the Relationship Circle? You get angry easily, you blame and hold resentments toward others, you are envious or narcissistic? Then you are reading the wrong chapter. If you remember from Chapter 3, the key to Working the Triangle is not to focus on what you are doing that is negative, but on what you are *not* doing that is positive! If you react in −Red you would be best served by integrating either some +Blue and/or +Yellow into your repertoire. In light of that, I would recommend that you take a look at the relevant parts of the Blue(Heart) and Yellow(Mind) chapters. If you react in the negative range of −Orange (−Red plus

–Yellow) I strongly recommend that you consider developing more reactions from the positive range of Blue(Heart). If you react in –Purple (–Red and –Blue) you would also benefit from reading the Yellow(Mind) chapter.

Working the Triangle: Red(Power)

I previously defined responsibility as the "ability to respond," not react. What are the effective ways to respond in Red(Power)? This is an important question to answer when we are attempting to Work the Triangle.

Take Zack as an example. He usually reacted with too much appeasement (–Blue) and then disconnection or avoidance (–Yellow) toward his controlling wife. In order for him to Work the Triangle, he needed to incorporate his missing movement: +Red. Most of his married life he had reacted to his wife with meager and desperate defensiveness—a very poor-quality –Red with not enough power to "get her attention." The general effect was merely to arouse her pain-body even more–making her more angry. However, he eventually learned to rise to occasions with enough high-grade +Red to bring him back into a dynamic balance; he found his "sweet spot." But what had kept him from integrating +Red in the first place? It was the same reason we all fail to integrate our "missing movement," fear and anxiety.

Ontological Fear or Anxiety

Ontological means "related to or based upon being or existence." I use it here to suggest that we all have basic anxieties originating from our relatively brief history on this planet. The ontological fear associated with Red(Power) is the anxiety related to being "bad." In other words, if we misbehave, act like a bully, or are mean to others we will be unaccepted in the group or tribe. We will be hated in return. This return hate or disapproval could affect a person's standing in the group, esteem that he might enjoy, and could perhaps even lead to his premature death. People who are afraid to act in Red(Power) are afraid of being bad or hurtful. This is a form of social guilt.

In Chapter 1, I discuss the concept of "witches," as it relates to pain-body. I define witches as those scary psychological or emotional parts of us.[6] Our Red witches are those parts of ourselves that are noxious if not terrifying in the Red(Power) dimension. And the experience of these Red witches tends to be shared— to a greater or lesser extent—with all humans. These witches are another version of pain-body—our un-integrated, negative psychological energy.

A very similar (if not identical) concept of the Red witch is what Carl Jung referred to as the *animus*. The *animus* is an archetype of the *collective unconscious* (an unconscious shared in some fashion by all human beings—in other words, ontological). Jung states that the *animus* is the "masculine"—or aggressive Red(Power)—part of the psyche that is unconscious and denied in the female. (I would suggest that it is also denied in men when we are less than courageous.) It is part of our journey, especially for females, to own and integrate our *animus*—our scary masculine—Red [Power]—side. In doing so we melt our Red witch, releasing vital and important energy that we need for optimal living.

Confounded in the Key of Red

There are many versions or manifestations of Red witches where we can be easily confounded. I will focus on just two: anger and conflict.

If anyone is going to successfully move through the Red(Power) dimension they will have to learn how to feel and deal with anger. Anger is a powerful emotion. For most people anger is a scary emotion. For survival it is a necessary emotion. Some might propose that we can avoid the experience of anger if we live in total harmony with the self and within the world. I doubt this very much. Anger happens! It is a normal part of limbic functioning and has been part of the human psyche for a very long time.

At this point it might be important to define our terms. You see, many people have an angry reaction to anger. They don't like anger. To them, anger is *always* a bad thing. One reason for this is because they think that anger is equivalent to hostility. It is true that all hostility involves anger, but not all anger is hostile. Our first experience with anger happens within seconds of our birth. We let out a blood-curdling scream that says, "Where am I? I don't like this! I was comfortable, I was warm, I was fed, and now what's happening?" Anger is the emotion of "not liking something." In fact, when I work with people who are not experienced with the emotion of anger, I will start them at that most basic

level. I will help them look at things they don't like
and see how their body reacts to that.

I recently supervised the case of a woman who
avoided any expression of anger. An important detail
of her history is that that her mother was sick with
cancer for most of her childhood, and died from the
cancer when the girl was still young. The girl tried
to help her mother but was of course unable to save
her. Any suggestion that she might be angry with her
mother for not being available through her childhood,
and for abandoning her at such a young age when she
died, seemed absurd. How could she possibly hold this
against her unfortunate mother, who never asked to
be sick? However, looking at it from another perspective, how could she possibly like the fact that losing
her mother so early in her life robbed her of the experience of having a loving, energetic mother to parent
her? This conflict around anger at her mom stunted
her grief process. Any grief process not only involves
feelings of sadness but also a natural sense of anger.
It was initially a scary journey when she was invited
to be upset with her mother for leaving her. However,
later it was liberating. The permission to feel the anger
allowed her to move through the grief process and on
with the rest of her life with an integrated and loving
memory of her mother.

This is only one example of many where experiencing anger can be scary (especially for one who tends
to be Blue or Yellow). Other examples include such
things as being angry with your boss, who could fire
you; your spouse, who might withhold love (or even

leave you); or your children, who conceivably might be damaged by your anger.

Related to anger is the issue of conflict. Many people are what we call "conflict avoidant." This is when we consciously or unconsciously go out of our way to circumvent a potential clash with another person or group. I understand this. It takes nerve to be +Red. Yet if we do not speak the truth as we know it, or ask for needs on our own behalf, the cost can be great. Accepting conflict earlier rather than later will often solve a problem with less stress for everyone than if we "put it off until another time."

In fact, in all the issues noted above, the ability to Work the Triangle involves having the courage to integrate the positive aspects of Red(Power). We just have to believe that being candid, setting a firm boundary, or being forceful about an important concern is an act of responsibility and will, in the long run, be best not just for ourselves but for the others involved as well.

Chapter 5

Moving Toward
and the Heart Dimension

I am love. I care for the well-being of Others. I respect, honor, and cherish Others. I am tuned in to who they are, where they are, and what they need. I belong. I am one with Others. I converge. I join. I fellowship and identify. I prefer "we" to "me." I attach. I need Others. I cannot stand alone. I need to be oiled with care, support, provisions, and expertise, all of which come from community. I hunt with the Others; we harvest food together. I parent children within a community and make decisions with Others for our common good. I say, "Yes, I am us."

Musings in the Key of Blue

Where the psychological orientation of Red(Power) is on Self, the psychological orientation of Blue(Heart) is on and about the Other. The Other is cared for and loved. The Other is honored and respected. We get up in the middle of the night to care for the Other (sick child). We stop on the way home to buy flowers for the Other (spouse). We go out of our way to say thank you to the hard-working Other (employee). We sincerely respect the Other (member of Congress) who sits on the opposite side of most issues that you believe in. A Christian embraces a Muslim, a Muslim respects a Jew, a straight person welcomes a gay person, a young person honors an older person. Yes, even the lion lies with the lamb.

As much as *Homo sapiens* are an aggressive species, we are a loving and caring species as well. We care for our young and we care for each other. Our capacity for aggression explains why we have become what we are on Earth today—with all our amazing advances and appalling violence. Our capacity for love is also why we become what we are on Earth today—with all our institutions that care for others and the sacrifices we make for those we love, and even for some we don't.

Divergence, Convergence, and Observance

In Chapter 4 we talked about how Red is divergent. In its positive manifestation, divergence articulates our uniqueness. A Democrat is different from a Republican in how they view issues such as taxation, income distribution, how to help the poor, the death penalty, and so on. "Black culture" is different from "White culture" in its music, food, and language. And I am uniquely different from you. In its negative manifestation, divergence is the basis of prejudice and hate. Democrats can detest Republicans; Republicans can detest Democrats. Blacks can be suspicious of Whites, and Whites can be suspicious of Blacks. And I can despise you because you are not like me.

It is the opposite for Blue. Blue(Heart) converges. Convergence defined is *a meeting*—becoming the same—arriving at the same destination and having similar characteristics.

Although our Ego would have us believe differently, we have much more in common than we have in contrast (and our +Blue knows this). We all exist in the tiny lifeboat called Earth as it bounces around in the gigantic ocean of the universe. We only have each other. We can either survive and thrive on this planet together or mutually destroy ourselves. And for the first time in our brief history we are technologically capable of destroying ourselves (along with many, if not all, other living creatures). But when we do work together we can do amazing things.

Quantum mechanics suggests that everything is essentially made up of the same thing: vibrating energy. And by "everything" I mean everything: rocks, trees, bacteria, insects, the president of the United States, massive stars, and your dog. We are essentially made of the same "stuff," just in slightly different forms. In that way we are all strangely connected to everything else, a circumstance that is very much in tune with that is Blue(Heart) dimension. We have all had the experience of enjoying nature (on the beach, in a forest, or even a desert) and have known the sensation of being at one with it. Many of us have also had the same feeling of connection, or unity, with people (and/or animals).

The Hindus use a greeting of highest respect, *Namaste* (pronounced nah-məs-tay). *Namaste* is usually spoken with a slight submissive bow and hands pressed together, palms touching and thumbs close to the chest. Namaste literally means, "I bow to the divine in you." This would be offensive to a Judeo-Christian-Muslim monotheistic worldview. But if you can get past the theology, it becomes a symbol and practice of recognition and respect for all that we have in common.

Just as there is a negative aspect of divergence (prejudice) there are also negative aspects of convergence—namely, enmeshment, codependency, and hypersensitivity. Enmeshment is a concept introduced by Salvador Minuchin to describe families where personal boundaries are diffuse, subsystems undifferentiated, and over-concern for others leads to a loss of autonomous development.[1] Enmeshment is when we converge so much that we lose ourselves in the process—unfortunately not in an energetic above-the-line way, but in a destructive, below-the-line space.

Related to enmeshment is the oft-used term *codependency*. Originally the term *codependent* meant literally co-dependent—"with a dependent." In other words, a codependent "enabled" another's addiction. So the husband who picked up wine on his way home from work for his alcoholic wife would be considered codependent. However, its meaning soon became generalized to mean any person whose caring was disproportionate. There is healthy (above-the-line, or high-grade) +Blue caring; and then there is codependency, an excessive (below-the-line/ low-grade) –Blue caring often at the cost of the individual's own autonomy and well-being. It is not a conscious (+Yellow) caring but knee-jerk compulsive taking care of others often at the codependent's expense. In fact, codependency has been referred to as the disease of a lost self.[2]

Whereas –Orange (–Red and/or –Yellow) is by definition "insensitive," Blue(Heart) is sensitive. This +Blue capacity to be sensitive to others and our environment is essential to successful living and creation of a viable society (see the next section on "Society"). And although it is vital that we are perceptive of others and our environment, all of us (some of the time) and some of us (most of the time) can be *too* sensitive. When this happens a person becomes touchy and easily hurt or offended—thin-skinned, if you will—rendering him or her reactive. This hypersensitivity can readily trigger the pain-body and Egoic reactions.

How does one tell when one's caring or sensitivity level is healthy or unhealthy? The answer to this question is true for most areas where we are looking for insight; it is about the energy. Does one's caring or level of sensitivity create positive, useful, fulfilling energy, or does it eventually *deplete* positive energy or create negative energy? To discern this requires conscious, mindful awareness (+Yellow).

It is probably becoming obvious that the goal is neither divergence nor convergence but the positive of both. In fact, in the spirit of Working the Triangle, it is the dynamic interaction between the two—uniqueness and unity—where we find the harmony and balance. And how do we know which to use at which time and to what degree? You'll need to ask Scarecrow (+Yellow) about that in the next chapter.

The Power of Love

If you have been to a wedding within the last 30 or 40 years, you've probably heard the following passage from the New Testament. I invite you to consider it again, but this time not with the bride or even with religion in mind but with your Blue hat on. Here it is, probably one of the most famous passages on love:

> If I speak in the [languages] of men or of angels, but do not have love, I am only a resounding gong or a clanging cymbal. If I have the gift of prophecy and can fathom all mysteries and all knowledge, and if I have a faith that can move mountains, but do not have love, I am nothing. If I give all I possess to the poor and give over my body to hardship that I may boast but do not have love, I gain nothing.

Love is patient, love is kind. It does not envy, it does not boast, it is not proud. It does not dishonor others, it is not self-seeking, it is not easily angered, it keeps no record of wrongs. Love does not delight in evil but rejoices with the truth. It always protects, always trusts, always hopes, always perseveres.

Love never fails.[3]

Based on this passage, love is the answer—to the woes of Chapter 4. It addresses, if not corrects, all that is troublesome about –Red.

So which below-the-line dimension (along with its associated behaviors) is the worst? Shall we take a vote? They are all negative; they all vibrate with low-grade, heavy, burdensome energy. They all produce miscommunication, disconnection, and adverse effects. But if there were only one dimension that we could amend, which one would you pick? Personally, I would pick –Red. It seems to me that the thing that we *Homo sapiens* just can't get control over is our (dis)ability to hurt each other. We've learned many good things in our sojourn on this planet, but how to deal with our anger and hatred is hardly one of them. When we think of the things in human history that we would consider most horrible, we might look at the Holocaust and suggest that the indifference of much of the world to the plight of the Jews and other victims of that atrocity would place negative behaviors in the Yellow dimension in the "most dangerous" category. But to my mind, the aggressive inhumanity of the Nazis in that example casts –Red in the prize-winning role for the most horrific dimension. Yet if Paul is right, love (+Blue) can triumph over the evils of (–Red).

Love is powerful in its own Blue(Heart) kind of way. Love brings out the best in people. Employee engagement and reinforcement of positive behaviors are shown to significantly raise worker productivity. Love works! Love wins! That is good. +Blue can make people work better. But can love fix the *big* stuff (like the ancient writer Paul might suggest)? Can love conquer racial prejudice and bigotry? Can it turn around the shameless and brutal ambition of dictators? Can love defeat ISIS? The answer is yes—sometimes . . . *and* eventually. It was Martin Luther King, Jr., who said, "The arc of the moral universe is long, but it bends towards justice." And he should know. His journey toward +Blue (and +Red and +Yellow) was long, very long. He only got to see the very beginning of the bend in the road toward recovery from shameless, mindless prejudice before someone violently took his precious life. He did not live long enough to see the more explicit changes in social policy, much less America's first Black president. And we will probably not be around long enough to witness categorical changes of the magnitude that would give us universal openness to people regardless of their race, religion, sexual orientation, and gender. But love is the quality that can bend that arch toward justice.

Dependency

The Other is not only cared for, the Other is also needed. When Dorothy, Toto, and Scarecrow first find

Tin Man, he is rusted—frozen in the forest, unable to move, helpless and hopeless. Observant Scarecrow realizes that Tin Man is in need of something that he is unable to give to himself; he needs to be oiled. The truth is we all need to be oiled. When we are sick as a child, we need a loving parent to care for us. We need to feel appreciated by our spouse, perhaps flowers for no good reason. And as an employee we need more than a paycheck; we need to feel appreciated for our hard work. And we all know that members of Congress need respect from one another.

Dependency is tricky. As much as we are called upon to take responsibility for ourselves, there are still many things we cannot do without the help of others. If you take time to think about it objectively, you'll realize how dependent we really are on other people. These everyday dependencies are interwoven so deeply into the fabric of our society, we hardly notice them until they are gone. We had unusually high winds blow through our neighborhood a few years ago, taking out the electricity for an entire week. I did not realize how dependent I was on electricity, heat, and hot water (it happened during late fall/early winter). But these types of dependencies are nothing in comparison to the emotional dependencies we have on each other. Being vulnerable leaves us, well, vulnerable.

In a previous book I went into detail on how to discern healthy (above-the-line) dependency from unhealthy (below-the-line) dependency. I suggested that if we can attain this state for ourselves then we should, and if we can't do it for ourselves, we should ask for help. But it is so more complicated than that. Sometimes having someone else do something for us—even if we *can* do it ourselves—is far superior. I can cook for myself but sometimes it is just nice if someone makes a meal for me. I can always rub my own foot, but I'd almost always prefer a professional foot rub. There is good reason for this. As Sarah-Jayne Blakemore and her colleagues found in a 1998 study using fMRI to measure activity in the brain's somato-sensory cortex, we feel sensation more intensely when a stimulus comes from someone else than when it is self-produced. This is one of the reasons it's nearly impossible for us to tickle ourselves. And we can extend this concept to other aspects of our interactions as well.

There are two potential errors we can make when it comes to dependency.

1. We may be too dependent. We ask or expect others to take care of us too much, too often, for too many things that we can do ourselves. This renders the dependent person truly weak and "needy." We've all met people like this. They are unsure of themselves and their decisions. They lack confidence. They look to others for constant direction and implementation. They lack positive +Red. (Or they see themselves as entitled to get things without working for them. They keep a ledger in their head and the world still owes them.)

2. We may not be dependent enough. We see dependency as weakness. Our Ego creates a narrative about dependency as a defect or

disadvantage, so we tough it out. (Imagine a Tin Man who would be damned if he let Dorothy oil him.) Yet we all have emotional and practical needs, and at times it can be enriching for all parties if we let others help us. Somewhere between these two errors we find the sweet spot, the healthy balance. It's a place where the Ego is quieted and wisdom (+Yellow) is employed. If we are going to live successfully, we have to give up our Egoic idea that "dependency is always weakness." Business leaders need to ask for feedback from their team. A spouse needs to ask for time to talk about something that is troubling them. A child needs to ask a teacher for help with something that they don't understand. And yes, men need to ask for directions when lost.

We also need wisdom to know the difference between healthy (above-the-line) dependency and unhealthy (below-the-line) dependency. This wisdom cannot be taught; it has to learned through trial and error. So if we tend to be too dependent, we need to take the risk of independence—even if we make mistakes. And if we tend to be too independent, we need to swallow our pride and ask for "oil."

The Place of Blue in Society
Cooperation, Collaboration, and Congregation

In the previous chapter I identified the key role of competition in the formation of our current society. I now offer an opposing role for Blue(Heart) in society: cooperation. Where competition is based on divergence, cooperation is based on convergence. We are pack animals (in the sense that we live in packs, not that we carry packs—although sometimes we do that too). As long as we've been "human" we've hunted together, gathered together, parented children together, played together, built together, created together, and fought together. When you think about what has allowed us to evolve and progress as much as we have as a species, our ability to cooperate plays a critical role.

Ed Bacon, author of *The Eight Habits of Love*,[4] is often known to say, "Love makes the human race into the human family." There is something about this simple statement that captures the essence of Blue's role in society. What do you think of when you think of "family"? In the best sense of the word, I think of togetherness, cooperation, and commitment. I also think of identification. People in a family see each other as being part of the same thing. Family members recognize each other. So next time you encounter someone who is "different" from you (by virtue of skin color, nationality, religion, or political persuasion), experiment with seeing them as members of the same community—the human family. Pull the camera back to get a wide-angle view of the other person. Try on convergence. See them as fellow sojourners in the same lifeboat—the one bobbing up and down in this gigantic ocean we call the universe.

This is not just a pleasant exercise. In his work *The Emotional Life of Your Brain*, Dr. Richard Davidson, along with Sharon Begley, explain what this kind of thinking can do for training compassion (in other words, developing +Blue). Davidson's research, based at the University of Wisconsin–Madison, focuses on the neural bases of emotion and emotion-related disorders such as anxiety and depression. A longtime friend of the 14th Dalai Lama, Richardson has had multiple opportunities to measure the brain activity of monks, as well as control groups, both before and after several types of meditation. His findings in terms of one form of meditation, known as "compassion meditation," offer valuable insights into the junction of compassionate +Blue with mindful +Yellow (together +Green). In compassion meditation, you start out thinking of someone you care about at a high level (significant other, parent, child) and imagine them in a sad or painful situation while strongly hoping for their freedom from suffering. You feel that feeling on a fundamental, meditative level, then expand it out circle by circle to your next ring of relationships and try to apply that same feeling to them until you can apply it to "all sentient beings." Fortunately, the results seen in brain scans (fMRI) of this "compassion meditation" show that we don't have to be a monk (having 10,000+ hours of this experience) to enjoy the benefits. That said, the more time we spend in this activity, the more effortless it becomes. Eventually it feels, as one subject put it, "like a total readiness to act, to help." The upshot is that you and I can, even with our limited schedules, train compassion. And the balanced brain that emerges from such training is more than simply good for society. It's crucial to human survival.

I have been trained as a mediator and as a collaborative law (or family law) coach. I use the skills that I have learned in organizations to help resolve conflict, and I use them also in divorce proceedings where I work collaboratively with a team that includes family lawyers and a financial advisor. Our current legal system, as it pertains to dispute resolution in general and divorce in particular, is based on litigation—fighting: Red divergence and competition. Most of the time the only "winners" in these cases are the lawyers, who run up the divorcing couple's bill and engender animosity and hate en route. Collaborative law is based instead on convergence. It appeals to logical and reasonable co-operation (healthy +Blue) between the divorcing couple. The mediators, collaborative lawyers, and neutral financial advisor all work together to help the divorcing couple converge on the most fair and "civilized" divorce for them and their family. Although this approach to dispute resolution is easier said than done, it sure beats the alternative: all-out war. It takes all parties being willing and able give up their Egoic, unhealthy –Red self-righteousness and interest in "winning" so they can collaborate together as reasonable people— and there's the rub. *Homo sapiens* naturally congregate; we come together and form identifiable units. One of the main things that I do as an organizational consultant is to help companies form and/or develop teams. One definition of a team is the coordinated effort of individuals toward a common goal. The trend in most organizations is to utilize teams quite intentionally. Why? Because no one individual can do it all, see it all, and implement it all by themselves. I like to give an assessment that measures team roles based on the work of Meredith Belbin. In his book *Management Teams*[5] he concludes, based on his extensive study of how team members interact, that an effective team's members cover nine key roles.[6] Of course, no one person is proficient in all nine roles. In fact, seldom does any one individual fulfill more than three of the roles well enough. The practical application for a work team, therefore, is to bring together members whose skills combine to cover them all. The implication for us is to deeply appreciate that no one person can do it all. So whether you are part of a hunting party in 8000 BC or an executive team in a Fortune 500 company, you will need the blended, coordinated capacities of each team member with their unique skills to work effectively.

Another aspect of a team is an implied common challenge, if not opponent—perhaps even an enemy— to be faced. Is it possible to have a team without an enemy? I'd like to think so, but even if we use the word *challenge* instead of *enemy*, we can often stand to change our focus as a society. When we stop seeing *one another* as the challenge and start focusing on the issues that we all face together (like poverty, disease, natural disasters, or environmental threats), then we can bring the best of competition and cooperation together—as a team!

Attachment

One of the great achievements in the understanding of human development has come from studies in human attachment. The basic tenet of attachment

theory is that an infant needs to have a secure, responsive (+Blue) relationship with at least one adult
to ensure the child's successful social and emotional
development. This is especially important for a child
to acquire the ability to regulate emotional states and
behaviors later in adulthood. People who have poor attachment relationships when they are young generally
have more pain-bodied anxiety, anger, loneliness, and
depression later in adult life and they have a harder
time regulating the extra pain-body they acquire.

Daniel Siegel, cofounder of the field of interpersonal neurobiology (IPNB), together with Alan Sroufe,
an eminent expert on early attachment relationships,
posted an informative paper on attachment called
"The Verdict Is In: The Case for Attachment Theory."
In this paper they give a very succinct review of attachment theory, including the results of a longitudinal
study by The Minnesota Longitudinal Study of Risk
and Adaptation (MLSRA). The MLSRA, a research
project begun in 1976, has been the source of a vast literature about the predictive power of early attachment
relationships. They conclude:

> In general, [the quality of] attachment pre-
> dicted engagement in the preschool peer group,
> the capacity for close friendships in middle
> childhood, the ability to coordinate friendships
> and group functioning in adolescence, and the
> capacity to form trusting, non-hostile romantic
> relationships in adulthood. Those with secure

histories were more socially competent and likelier to be peer leaders. Each of these findings, as well as the findings on [increased] resilience and [reduced] psychopathology to be discussed, holds true controlling for temperament and IQ.[7]

The findings from this longitudinal study on the importance of human attachment are nothing short of astounding. If we want a society full of decent, balanced people we want to do everything we can to enhance early life attachments.

In the same article, Siegel and Sroufe refer to Dr. Mary Ainsworth, colleague of the founder of attachment theory, John Bowlby. Known for her breakthrough research in mother–infant observation during the 1960s, Ainsworth made a distinction between three types of attachment, later expanded to four. In the first type, *secure attachment,* children are able to explore their surroundings but return to the attachment figure when anxious or in need of comfort. The other three types are *insecure* types, each with their own signatures and categorized as avoidant, ambivalent, or disorganized attachment. Children who were securely attached were comfortable and proactive in reconnecting with their caregiver even when the caregiver stressed them. It is important to note that even the best parents are only accurately in tune with their child about half the time. The critical occurrence in a child becoming securely attached has more to do with how the caregiver and baby make up, that is, repair the rupture that ensues when there is a failure in empathy. On the other hand, an insecurely attached child—after repeated failures to repair—will either avoid the care-giver and/or is unable to be soothed.

Many books have been written on the history, the tenets, and the benefits of early (and later) attachment and the problems associated with insecure attachment styles. It is enough to say here that we are wired to need connection with supportive, responsive others—to be loved (oiled) from infancy until we die. This includes being protected. Little, furry, baby mammals protect-ed themselves by instinctively running into a hole or a burrow. On the other hand, primate babies ran—so to speak—into their mothers' arms. No one that I know thinks we ever outgrow our need for attachment. In fact, beginning in the 1980s, other researchers gradu-ally expanded Bowlby's and Ainsworth's studies to the point that there is robust evidence in the literature de-scribing how attachment styles between adults also in-fluence how we cope with our emotions, our self, and our interactions with others. Beyond doubt, through-out life we will always need someone who will be there when we are scared or confused, and especially when we need to repair a rupture in our emotional world.

The Morality of Blue

It was a hard sell to show the morality of Red, but I am hopeful that Chapter 4 made it evident there are many positive aspects of Red(Power). Selling the mo-rality of Blue(Heart) is easier. In our society, matters of the Heart are often seen as positive. Once again I draw your attention to the top half of the Relationship Circle, this time to the items in +Blue. Any and all of these attitudes and behaviors are positive, lifegiving, communication enhancing, and good outcome producing. Here are a few positive attributes of Blue(Heart) that I'd like to note:

Golden Rule

We all know the "Golden Rule." It goes something like this: Treat others as you would have them treat you. (The reciprocal is to not treat others as you would not like to be treated.) Many attribute this maxim of "moral reciprocity" to the Bible. And that would be true, except that this concept appears prominently in most religions, including Islam, Hinduism, Buddhism, Judaism, and Zoroastrianism.[8] It is easy to appreciate that this universal code of ethics keeps civilization civilized. Without a deep regard for the needs of others, society would not exist in any way that is remotely tolerable yet alone functional. Just as they have a Code Blue in the hospital when someone is having a cardiac (Heart) arrest, we should have a Code Blue in society whenever a Congressman maligns another, or the next door neighbor plays loud music at 2:00 a.m., or a boss impatiently yells at an employee, or a spouse mindlessly blames a partner for everything that ever troubled them.

We also know the Golden Rule in the form of "Love your neighbor as yourself," found in the parable of the Good Samaritan. Jesus tells of a man who was mugged, beaten, and left for dead on the road while on a journey to Jericho. Several upstanding religious leaders passed him along the road thinking it best to not get involved. But it was a Samaritan who saw the man, took pity, cared for his wounds, and transported him to an urgent care facility (of sorts) picking up the medical bills himself. The story is even more compelling knowing that Samaritans were an unpopular if not maligned class of people in that society.

The profundity of this moral directive is clearly +Blue in nature. It is convergence at its best—where "my neighbor" is really just another "me," we are all part of the same whole, worthy of being treated with utmost regard and care. Certainly we can connect to this idea when we hear in the news that ISIS is ready to behead another innocent victim. It is easily clear to us why they should listen carefully for Allah's Code Blue and base their behavior not on some radical hatred toward the West but on whether they would like someone to brutally take off their head or that of their child. It is harder to connect to this idea, however, when thinking about things we do to one another on a daily basis. Nevertheless, just as ISIS figuratively beheads everyone (even themselves) each time they literally behead one individual, likewise we "behead" someone (and everyone) each time we attack, envy, belittle, put down, resent, gossip, deny, offend, or blame our "neighbors." In a deep spiritual sense because we are all connected, we are also doing these things to everyone, including ourselves. Our hope for overcoming these tendencies and living by the Golden Rule lies in strengthening above-the-line qualities in the Blue dimension.

Empathy and Compassion

If there is one capacity that is essential to being +Blue it is the capacity for empathy. Simply stated, empathy is the ability to understand in a deep way the thoughts, feelings, and emotions of another person or group. It goes beyond the mimicking of words or mere intellectual prospecting of the other's experience. It is, as the Native American saying goes, "walking a mile in someone else's moccasins." Empathy is fundamental to good communication.

It is imperative as a speaker that I have empathy, so I can sense whether my audience is following me. It is crucial as a parent that I can "tune in" to the unspoken needs of my 2-year-old, so I can adequately help her navigate a difficult emotional crisis. It is essential as a leader that I am privy to the needs of my team, so they feel understood and respected. This tuned-in aspect of empathy is another form of Heart convergence.

Back in the late 20th century, a group of Italian neuroscientists headed by Giacomo Rizzolatti and Vittorio Gallese "discovered" what has come to be called *mirror neurons* found primarily in primates. These neurons get their name from the fact that they fire not only when we perform an action ourselves, but also when we see someone else perform the same action. Mirroring neurons are found in various parts of the brain, and although there is speculation about the full extent of their function, the prevailing understanding is that they have much to do with human empathy, as well as, perhaps, human language and other functions related to the ability to interpret intention in others.

These capacities are obviously vital to the functioning of any species that exist in complex societies, and no species on earth is more complex than the society of the *Homo sapiens.*

By the way, guess who is not good at empathy? If you said narcissists, you are correct. While studies show they are capable of empathy under certain conditions, narcissists are by design and dysfunction mostly tuned in to the self. Actually being tuned in to oneself can be beneficial as long as it is not at the expense of being accurately aware of others. I say "accurately" because narcissists are very cognizant of others but primarily through the prism of their own Egoic needs and interests. They experience others mostly in terms of their own personal utility. (This is why when someone does not directly or immediately meet his or her needs, a narcissist will often become irritated if not enraged.) They do not truly understand the separate and unique thoughts, feelings, and emotions of another person or group. This makes them ineffective—if not defective—as parents, leaders, friends, congressmen and members of society.

On the other hand, far, far away in another galaxy, there are those who "overdo" empathy, so to speak. Empathy overdone is similar to what we called enmeshment earlier in the chapter. And related to enmeshment is the phenomenon of *absorption.* People who overdo empathy (or, if you will, sympathy) fall into below-the-line, or −Blue. They tend to absorb everything around them, including the bad vibes of other people. They are like a pain-body sponge. So if your mother (or your spouse or your boss) is in their pain-body, their pain-body will soon be in you, if you tend to overdo empathy. You will absorb their emotion like a sponge soaks up liquid. It will then wreak havoc in your psyche and your body. You will feel bad and badly. You are likely to feel responsible in some way for the other person's distress.

People with this –Blue tendency become like a psychological toilet for the emotional waste products of others. Often another person will actually feel relieved after they "dump" on (or in) you, if you tend toward –Blue in this way. In fact, they will often seek you out to "share their feelings." But even when it is not intentional, the Blue-sponge will absorb it all the same. I had one client who was so "empathic," she literally became sick after hearing about a tragic earthquake in South America. This went beyond natural empathy for the suffering of others. She absorbed their suffering in her body. This is an extreme example of what many (if not all) –Blue individuals do: They absorb suffering and anxiety. As you might imagine, this is a vocational hazard for anyone in the helping professions (like therapists, nurses, clergy, or parents). But truth be told, it is a hazard for anyone trying to live a full harmonious life.

Service and Sacrifice

Serving the needs of others is not only a societal duty, it is a necessity for our own personal well-being. Caring about the needs of others not only benefits the receiver of the service but also the one serving. As it turns out, serving others is part of our "dharma" or design as human being. Numerous studies demonstrate that we function better physically as well as mentally when we are giving to others, and several—including a 2008 study conducted by Stephanie Brown and her colleagues at the University of Michigan—found that older people who spend a significant portion of their week caring for others can even enjoy prolonged lives as a result. We are "made" to care for and about each other. And society depends on the fulfillment of this need to serve others.

This is the basis of a principle you will find in all 12-step programs. If you are tempted to act out (drink, gamble, overeat, look at porn), be of service to someone. When the addict turns his or her attention away from the battle raging within their limbic system and looks to the needs of others in the program instead, they become relatively free from the cravings. To serve the needs of others gets us "out of ourselves" for a while and fulfills our Blue design. This results in yielding more internal harmony, not to mention creating a better society. The narcissist in us all thinks it is a zero-sum game. The more we receive, the more we get, while the more we give, the more depleted we are. There is nothing further from the truth.

No doubt you've heard the parable of the man who arrives in hell after dying. He opens the door into a large banquet room where he sees a sizable table loaded with an assortment of delicious nurturing food. All the people in the room have long forks fixed to their arms. In fact, the forks are too long to physically reach their mouths. As a result, we have a room of anguished people slowly dying of starvation because of their inability to feed themselves. This same man then goes to an adjacent room, labeled "Heaven." To his surprise, it is an identical room with an identical food-laden banquet table and extra-long forks attached to everyone's arms. Only in this room each person is feeding another. This sentimental parable depicts the mutual benefit of our feeding and serving each other and its importance to achieving a great society and sustaining the human family.

This Blue(Heart) attribute includes the concept of self-sacrifice. This comes into play when offering a service truly costs the server in time, money, pain, or risk to his or her own well-being. Any parent who gives up a trip to Europe to pay for their child's education, or the employee who stays past quitting time to complete a project without pay, or the neighbor who gives up a day off to help an elderly person next door is each practicing a +Blue type of selfless sacrifice. The young men and women who serve in our armed forces are exceptional examples of this. They literally risk their lives to protect their fellow citizens and our (we hope, legitimate) national interests.

Many police cars have written under their logo the phrase *To serve and to protect*. Perhaps if we all fancied ourselves to be police cars with that phrase prominent in our self-view, our world would be a much better place. Paradoxically, a right and proper love of self would also contribute to making the world a much better place.

Self-Love

I frankly did not know where to put this one. Should self-love go in the Red(Power) chapter with its focus on the self, or in this chapter—with its focus on the heart? Well, you can see where I decided to put it. I guess love wins again!

To me, "self-love" is the implicit, unconditional positive regard and grace one has toward oneself. It is an uncompromising attitude of care and concern for the only person we will be with our entire life: our self. Self-love is not to be confused with selfishness, which is common to all of us and especially those of us who are narcissistic by nature. In fact, I will argue that narcissists actually do not truly and deeply love themselves. If they did they would be secure and therefore would not have to be so damn self-centered. No, self-love is above the line (whether you put it in the Blue section or the Red section), and it is essential to harmonious living and personal happiness. However, for most of us who did not have a secure attachment and good genetics, self-love will often require "radical self-acceptance."

Dialectical behavior therapy, or DBT, is a modified form of cognitive-behavioral therapy (CBT) developed by Dr. Marsha Linehan. DBT combines standard CBT techniques for emotional regulation and reality testing with concepts of distress tolerance, acceptance, and mindful awareness (Yellow) largely derived from Buddhist meditative practice. Linehan endorses a practice called *Radical Acceptance.*[9] When confronting a problem you have four choices: You can either solve the problem, change how you feel about the problem, stay miserable or "radically accept" it as it is. By "radical" she means complete and total without conditions. So Radical Self-Acceptance means a complete and total acceptance of oneself regardless of our defects—real or imagined. It is a commitment to love ourselves regardless and no matter what. It is the truest and deepest expression of grace (and if necessary, forgiveness). (Please note: In the unlikely event that a sociopath is reading this, radical self-acceptance is not a license to be –Red ass.) I have found this +Blue attitude and commitment toward ourselves to be an extremely helpful practice for clients that I work with (and to be honest, for myself as well). Try it, you'll like it—and it will love you.

Blue Reactions
What if You Are a Blue Reactor?

What if you have a tendency to react in –Blue where you easily get enmeshed with others, absorb their pain-body, or keep poor boundaries? What if you find yourself too often in the below-the-line Blue portion of the Relationship Circle? You catch yourself feeling less than, if not inferior to, others? You are often immobilized, helpless—perhaps hopeless— or depressed and it seems the only way you can get your way is to manipulate people by guilt. Then you are reading the wrong chapter. If you remember from Chapter 3, the key focus of Working the Triangle is not on what you are doing that is negative (--Blue), but on what you are *not* doing that is positive! If you react in –Blue you would be best served to integrate either some +Red and/or +Yellow into your repertoire. In light of that, I would recommend that you take a look at the relevant parts of the Red(Power) and Yellow(Mind) chapters. If you react –Green (–Blue and –Yellow), I strongly recommend that you consider +Red. If you react in –Purple (–Blue and –Red) I recommend the Yellow(Mind) chapter. See you there.

Working the Triangle: Blue(Heart)

The thesis of this book suggests that it is not about what we are doing that is unhealthy or wrong but what we are *not* doing that is healthy and "right." In light of this chapter, what are the effective ways to respond in +Blue? This is an important question to answer when we are attempting to Work the Triangle. One way to explore this is to understand what the basic fears are that we tie to the Blue(Heart) dimension that keeps us from incorporating +Blue behaviors into our relational repertoire.

Ontological Fear or Anxiety

As we learned in Chapter 4, ontological fears are those related to or based upon our relatively brief history on earth. If you recall, the ontological fear associated with Red(Power) is the anxiety related to being "bad" and thus rejected from the tribe. The ontological fear associated with Blue(Heart) is different. It is the fear of being weak or vulnerable. In other words, if we let our guard down, if we submit, agree, or adapt, we think of ourselves as weak or disadvantaged. As a result of this "weakness" we are at the mercy of others, even if we're not in physical or psychological danger.

This is the fear held by the narcissistic personality. As you remember, the dirty little secret of narcissists is that they actually are exceedingly insecure and harbor a hidden narrative about themselves that is unflattering—often fending off feelings of being defective. So they spend their whole life hiding from this potential realization by fortifying a grandiose self-image and superior, if not invincible, portrayal of themselves.

Remember the Cowardly Lion from *The Wonderful Wizard of Oz*? His dirty little secret was not so secret when he was tested on the Yellow Brick Road. His true demeanor became obvious. After all the bravado was gone, he was a coward after all. This is true for any narcissist. Being true Blue(Heart) is too scary for them. They are genuinely afraid of their own (Blue) shadow.

In Chapter 1, I discuss the concept of "witches," as it relates to pain-body. I define witches as those scary psychological parts of us arising from deep-seated emotion–notions. Our Blue witches are those parts of ourselves that are noxious if not terrifying in the Blue(Heart) dimension. And the experience of these Blue witches tends to be shared—to a greater or lesser extent—with all humans. We are all terrified of being like Tin Man, frozen in the forest, unable to defend ourselves, and vulnerable to whims of those who would hurt us when we are in a weak space.

A very similar (if not identical) concept of the Blue witch is what Carl Jung referred to as the *anima*. The *anima* is an archetype of the *collective unconscious* (an unconscious shared in some fashion by all human be-ings—in other words, ontological). Jung states that the *anima* is the "feminine" (or vulnerable) part of the psyche that is unconscious and denied in the male. (I would sug-gest that it is also denied in women when they are less than vulnerable, as is the case with Betty in Chapter 3). It is part of our journey—especially for males—to own and integrate our *anima*, our scary feminine side, and in so doing melt our Blue witch, thus releasing vital and impor-tant energy that we need for optimal living.

Confounded in the Key of Blue

In just the same way one can be confounded in Red, we can also be confounded or confused between what is healthy +Blue and unhealthy –Blue. This is particularly true for –Orange (–Red and/or –Yellow) re-actors. They think Blue(Heart) in general is weak.

Vulnerable or Defenseless?

Vulnerable means to be open, without defense. This one meaning can have two outcomes. One outcome of being vulnerable is being harmed. The other outcome of being vulnerable is convergence, deep connection, getting real needs met, reconciling with another, and/or intimacy. The person who has a difficult time doing Blue(Heart) is unwilling (or terrified) to risk openness out of fear of being harmed.

There are conflicting theories about the origin of the handshake. The one that I like goes like this: Before written history, when two strangers met and ap-proached, they would each take their hand from their sword and clasp the hand of the other. This was an act of mutual vulnerability. Each left himself open to potential harm for the higher good of peace and civility. They took a risk and rendered themselves momentarily defenseless. If we ever hope to have intimacy, to reconcile with another person (or group or political party) or have real needs met, we will at some point have to open ourselves up to the possibility of getting hurt. Now, I am not advocating stupidity. If every time you open yourself up to someone they exploit you, then stop being vulnerable to that person. (It is ultimately your responsibility to protect yourself.) However, if you are *always* protecting yourself in a relationship, you can go nowhere but unhealthy –Red or –Yellow. So, if you ever expect to grow in your relationships, you just might have to take your hand off your sword and shield and take the emotional risk of being vulnerable. You just might have to say that you are sorry; or tell an employee how much you appreciate his work; and for goodness sake, tell your partner that you love him or her.

I worked with a woman who grew up with a narcissistic mother and an alcoholic father. A relative sexually abused her when she was little. As she was very attractive, many men pursued her and she exploited this at will. However, when she met her soul mate, she froze like Tin Man in the forest. Every time he opened himself up to her she repelled his approach and ran for the hills. She could not bring herself to tell him how much she liked him—even loved him. Being vulnerable was just too risky. She could get hurt—again.

Sad or Depressed

Sadness is the natural emotional response to loss and limits. If we lose a game, a job, a parent, a contract, a spouse—we naturally feel sad. If we confront limits, we can feel sad as well. For example, we can't be in two places (or with two spouses or in two careers) at the same time. Sadness duly felt is an important and necessary human emotion. It is unavoidable because there is no shortage of limitation and loss. We experience these conditions every day in some small way; and on some days we may experience them in very large ways (for example, when a loved one dies). Sadness is a truly deep human emotion and because of this it resides predominately in the above-the-line +Blue dimension. But it is a painful emotion, and because of this the Ego is often deployed to protect us from experiencing sadness. But this "protection" comes at a great psychological cost. We numb it with our favorite addictions (a sip of some alcohol, a peek at some porn, a binge on some tasty treats). Or we employ one of the main defenses against sadness: mania. The tactic used in mania is to move too fast—emotionally, relationally, or psychologically—to feel the sadness. In other words, we work too much, play too hard, talk too fast—and we never slow down to actually feel. All these Egoic defenses are costly to our soul, our relationships, our bodies, and the communities that we live in. The best way to deal with sadness is simply to feel it. Feel it to heal it.

People who are confounded in the Blue(Heart) dimension can often confuse sadness with depression.

These states are very different. Depression is based on the two Hs: helpless (powerless, no agency) and hopeless (despair). Depression is giving up, giving in, and giving over. It is void of useful energy. There are hundreds of books written on how to deal with depression. It is enough for our purposes to say that introducing some healthy +Red (Power and agency attitudes and behaviors) along with +Yellow (Mindfulness and containment) can make a big difference.

Humble or Humiliated?

Once again words like humble can carry more than one connotation. In its best +Blue meaning it is the opposite of arrogance and haughty superiority (−Red). On the other hand, some people who are confounded by Blue(Heart) confuse this with being inferior to others in rank and esteem.

One of the great (but seldom told) stories about Jesus was when he washed his disciples' feet.[10] On the night before he was executed he got out a tub of water and washed the feet of the people who meant the most to him. This seems a strange behavior unless you realize that most people in those days wore sandals and walked on dirt roads. It was a common gesture of hospitality for the servants of the house to wash a visitor's feet. On this night, however, it was not the hired servant or slave who washed their feet but the master himself. He humbled himself. He then instructed his disciples (or students) to do likewise with each other. Healthy humility is not thinking yourself so important that it would diminish you to wash the feet of someone you love, a stranger that you just met, or even at times an "enemy."

Ownership/Acknowledgment

As I mentioned earlier, one of the most important ingredients in the success of any relationship is the ability of both parties to acknowledge that their poop stinks. And do you know what? My poop stinks and so does yours. We all make mistakes, have pain-body eruptions, and get out of balance. We are, after all, humans, and therefore imperfect. The couples, executives, and friends that are the most dynamic (and least destructive) get this, and can appropriately acknowledge their shortcomings. Earlier in the chapter, I talked about the need to face our inner witches (the scary parts of ourselves) and when we do, they melt like Dorothy's green-faced hag. When we own our vulnerabilities and shortcomings with candor and grace, we can learn to live with them without shame.

For all of us sometimes, and some of us much of the time, we need to integrate healthy +Blue in order to Work the Triangle. This will require a clarity or discernment between healthy +Blue and unhealthy –Blue. We need to see that healthy +Blue is not weakness but—quite the contrary—is very powerful. Love is especially powerful for those who think it is not. There is nothing more impressive than when an arrogant person sincerely humbles him- or herself to say, "I was wrong." The earth shakes when that happens. Everyone and everything stops when a proud person shows humility. You can hear a pin drop.

In order for us to find balance in any and all our relationships we have to overcome our fears. To incorporate healthy +Blue, we have to transcend our anxious fear of being vulnerable or weak and take the high road of heart and love.

Chapter 6

Moving Away
and the Mindfulness Dimension

I am the Knower. I am Mindfulness. I pay attention. I am Awareness. I see without worry or judgment what is, as it is. I accept things as they are. I watch my own insanity and the insanity of others with a calm eye. I am the truest part of myself. I am self-control. I am the prefrontal cortex. I am master of my "monkey-mind," my "lizard-brain," and urges. I am Presence. I live in the here and now, the moment as it is for what it is. I see the Other and I see my Self—how we are the same and how we are different. I am science. I look at things

from afar. I am curious. I know when to "not know."
I do not say "yes." I do not say "no." I am Wisdom.

Musings in the Key of Yellow

Where the psychological orientation of Red(Power) is about Self and the psychological orientation of Blue(Heart) is about the Other, the psychological orientation of Yellow(Mind) is about neither. Yellow's orientation is about *knowing*, impartial to the interest and desires of self or others.

L. Frank Baum's Scarecrow wonderfully depicts this aspect of the Yellow(Mind) dimension. If you recall, Dorothy met Scarecrow at a crossroad on the Yellow Brick Road. She did not know which way to go. Yellow(Mind) is about both knowing *and* not knowing—but I get ahead of myself. The Scarecrow was made of straw, which rendered him impervious to pain, unaffected by hunger, and invulnerable to weather and whatever else might otherwise affect him. There is only one thing that threatened Scarecrow: fire (which we will talk about later in this chapter). Scarecrow is uninfluenced by self-interest or other-concern, and because of his resulting immunity to hurt and lack of desire he stands in a unique position to know things as they are. This makes him a great observer.

Divergence, Convergence, and Observance

In previous chapters we discussed how Red(Power) diverges from others and Blue(Heart) converges with others. Well, Yellow(Mind) does neither; instead it *observes* others. Yellow moves away from the pressure to either converge or diverge and instead simply knows in the moment. Please note I used the phrase *moves away*. This, of course, is the idea that Karen Horney used to designate our third and final dimension, which we call Yellow(Mind). In order to know something, in order to be mindful, one has to "move away" from it as the Observer or the Witness Within. The Yellow ability to move away to observe and "know," more than any other dimension of interpersonal movement, seems to distinguish us from other animals on this planet. The degree to which other mammals (such as primates, dolphins, or dogs) are conscious of themselves is unknown to me, but there seems to be a categorical difference in our ability to self-reflect and be self-conscious.

Some might argue—as I do—that this Observer or Witness Within is in fact our truest self, unimpeded by all that distracts and distorts in the name of self-interest and other concern. This is because our inner Observer, like Scarecrow, is impervious to pain, biases, and the emotion–notions that we've acquired over our lifetime. You see, our mind is host to numerous "foreign objects." It is host to numerous emotion–notions or stories about "me and my world." These emotionally charged narratives:

- ⋏ Are mostly semiconscious if not entirely subconscious; but . . .

- ⋏ Are very powerful. They are emotionally charged and can create strong mental states and moods;

⅄ Are often distorted, if not out-right false;

⅄ Are manic depressive. In other words, they exaggerate in either a negative direction ("I will never amount to anything") or an idealistic directions (e.g., "I am better than most people"); and they

⅄ Work in conjunction with our pain-body and Ego.

However, the Witness Within is free of these distorted emotion–notions—able to observe what is—without shame, blame, or guilt. It is for this reason I suggest that this Observer is our truest self. So when the question arises, "Who am I?" I would suggest that the sincere and curious part of the self that asks the question is in fact closer to who we are than the part of us that attempts to answer it. Ironically, the part of ourselves that strives to answer the question is not as in touch with who we are as the part of us that just does not know!

And that illustrates one of the great paradoxes of Yellow(Mind). In order to "know" something we often have to "not know" first. In fact non-knowing—suspending all previous assumptions and emotion–notions—is sometimes the only way to get to a deeper level of knowing. This is the "beginner's mind."[1]

Understanding this idea transformed how I did therapy. As a young therapist I had the faulty notion (or narrative) that I should have insight—if not answers—for most if not all of my clients' concerns. As the presumed "expert," I actually believed that I should always know what is going on with a client. It was only when I realized the folly of my alleged wisdom, and when I extended grace to myself for my lack of omniscience, that I gave myself permission to "not know," to be lost, to be a beginner. It was when I let myself go through the discomfort (and it is still uncomfortable) to not know, that I found new and important connections with the client. This is not only true when working with clients, but in most areas of my life. I recommend this approach to you. Next time you come to an intersection—like Dorothy did on the Yellow Brick Road—and you don't know which way to go, let yourself "not know." Gently stay in the empty space, unashamed and curious, wondering if and when a connection might come.

As early as 3000 BCE, with the dynamic contributions of the Egyptians, the Phoenicians, the Greeks, and finally the Romans, human society made a notable advance in Red(Power) dominion over the earth. We went from tribal clans to sophisticated societies. We made categorical progress in human agency with numbers, inventions, and advances in architecture, science, and engineering, among other accomplishments. Later with the introduction of monotheism (Judaism, Christianity, and later Islam) more than 2,000 years ago, and Buddhism even earlier, the importance of Blue(Heart)—love and grace—offered a similar categorical leap for human society. (You would not know this by the behavior many religious leaders have shown since then.) Clearly our efforts to assert the human will and productivity—Red(Power)—have been more successful than our ability to get along with each other and demonstrate true cooperation and kindness. We have been able to build beautiful cathedrals better than we have lived up to the principles of grace, heart, compassion, and love that the cathedrals represented. Nevertheless, the teaching of these qualities has become part of the human fabric. Now, 2,000 years later, the time for Yellow(Mind) has come. With the development of psychology at the beginning of the 20th century, neuroscience at the end of the 20th century, and the reintroduction of Eastern philosophies such as Buddhism, the world is on the cusp of a new age of Awareness. It is an age where human beings are working to find the balance between Power and Heart through Mindfulness. This mindfulness comes on many levels:

⅄ On a personal level, with more "enlightened" emotionally intelligent individuals.

⅄ On a spiritual level, where our relationship to the world, the unworldly, and God (however we accept or don't accept God) is impacted by our connection to the Observant Knower or Witness Within.

⅄ On an organizational level, with a growing interest in organizational culture, and employee and client engagement, and with an increase in the number of psychologically healthy workplaces.

⅄ On a geopolitical level, with governmental organizations able to transcend petty differences and ideologies to solve real human needs.

It is a time for people to harness the power of Presence.

The Power of Presence

This section is perhaps one of the more important sections in the book, and I am hard pressed to write about it because I am only a beginner. I am only starting to understand how to tap into the profound power of mindfulness in my own life. And yet to the degree that I have practiced it, I have found a personal and interpersonal transformation. I am coming to believe that the power and practice of Presence is a necessary step in dealing with our pesky—and all too often destructive—emotion–notions, reactive pain-body, and Ego.

Perhaps one of the best ways to describe and prescribe mindfulness is to reflect on several interrelated aspects of this complex concept. The ideas that I talk about below might seem similar to each other because they are. They are all facets of the same jewel: mindfulness.

Observance → Awareness → Consciousness

We've already discussed the idea of the inner Observer—the Witness Within, which describes that seemingly unique human capacity to move away from an emotionally charged event, whether interpersonal in nature or not, and be witness of it rather than a reactor to it. This allows us to eventually be in control of the person that we need to control most, our self.

When we are able to observe, we become aware. Awareness, by definition, is the feeling, the experiencing, or the noticing of what *is*.[2] There are many in the field of psychology, including me, who believe that awareness is not only one of the key ingredients of mental health, it is, more importantly, the *means* by which we become mentally and emotionally healthy. I often say that awareness is at least 51 percent of the solution, and without awareness personal change is often not possible. Awareness is one of the essential ingredients of emotional intelligence—the awareness of oneself and the awareness of others. It's important to note that awareness is categorically more than knowledge or even insight. You can know about or have an insight into something without being aware. Awareness is born out of knowing "what is" and not through studying or making intellectual connections. And unlike knowledge and insights, awareness leads to consciousness.

Consciousness is related to and a byproduct of awareness. Consciousness carries with it the idea of total psychological perception. It is being totally awake and alert. This ability to be conscious of others and ourselves on whatever level is available to us again suggests to me something that truly distinguishes us from other animal forms on earth. And this experience of what we call consciousness can be a remarkable state of mind. There is a Sanskrit word, *Satcitnanda*, which is actually a word comprised of three words. "Sat" has as its root the idea of pure and timeless essence or being. "Cit" means consciousness, understanding, and knowing. "Ananda" means happiness or joy. Put together, *Satcitnanda* expresses something like the sublime experience of consciousness. This might come across to some as Eastern mumbo-jumbo, but if you have ever known this state, you will appreciate that it describes perhaps one of the more important "spiritual" experiences that we can have as human beings.

Presence

Presence is consciousness within time. Presence conveys the idea of being *fully there* in the moment— fully alert. You are not stuck in the past nor jumping ahead into the future. You are there in the *here and now*. The key difference between healthy, above-the-line, high-quality +Yellow and unhealthy, below-the-line, low-quality –Yellow is measured in large part by the degree that you are present with and conscious of the other person and/or especially yourself.

Acknowledge, Accept, and Allow (AAA)

This facet of mindfulness describes our capacity to acknowledge "what is" and then accept and/or allow that it *is* what it is. This is the "AAA" of mindfulness. So often we emotionally resist "what is" instead of acknowledging it and accepting it or allowing it. It is important to note that when I suggest "acceptance" I am not sanctioning passivity (lack of agency); I am endorsing recognizing what is true in the moment. Nor is acceptance a form of giving up, but rather it is giving *in* to what is. In fact, acceptance often puts us in a position where we can ultimately find true agency. So if you are unemployed, lost, feeling ill, have negative self-esteem, in physical pain, have a mental illness, were abused as a child, in a bad marriage, in a good marriage . . . acknowledge and accept it. And when we acknowledge "what is" and accept it rather than denying it, numbing it, fighting it, or "acting it out," we can *allow* the experience of it. So if you are angry, sad, scared, or even happy, acknowledge it and allow it to be in you as it is—even if it is an uncomfortable feeling. If you do, you will create space.

Spaciousness

In a lecture given in 2004, Eckhart Tolle talked about spaciousness. This is the gist of what he said:

> There comes a point where you get the first glimpse of "I can't fight it anymore." I can't fight what is, so I might as well accept what is. And suddenly there is space! With the simple [act] of accepting "what is now," suddenly there is a space around that which you accept. Before there was no space around the events . . . no space around reactions, no space around thoughts . . . and suddenly when you surrender to what is, there is a sense of depth in you. There is the event . . . the thought, the emotion, anger, sadness the story in the head . . . And suddenly there is space around it through simple acceptance.[3]

This idea of creating space around our reaction to an event through AAA revolutionized how I thought about and practiced mindfulness. So instead of avoiding, resisting, or numbing my experiences, I try to simply acknowledge, accept, and allow what is. And when I do, I create space around it. When we create this spaciousness, our reactions are mindfully mediated as a result. For example, if you are sad, instead of fighting the sadness simply acknowledge the sadness and accept that you are sad now. Surrender to the fact of your sadness, allow yourself to feel sad, and watch the space form around it, making it now more manageable. This is mindfulness. When this happens the Witness is engaged rather than the "antagonists" in our story. We are Observers and not reactors. Try this a few times; you will be amazed.

There is an immense power in being mindful as described by the attributes and practices we have discussed. Mindfulness is the clutch when shifting the gears from reactivity to response-ability. And that is why I think of Yellow(Mind) as the Master Mode.

The Master Mode

Although I experience my children differently, I love and respect them equally. I see their uniqueness, but I do not see one as more important to me than the other. And as much as I want to have the same disposition with the three dimensions of relating interpersonally, I cannot. Even as Dorothy seemed to favor Scarecrow, I have come to the conclusion that cultivating our Yellow(Mind) is of utmost importance for our future as individuals and as a society. Considering *The Wonderful Wizard of Oz* again, at the end of the book, Glinda asks Scarecrow (not compassionate Tin Man or King Lion) to replace the Wizard to rule over the Emerald City, the executive center of the Land of Oz. Why would that be?

There is something that is transcendent about consciousness.

As much as I wanted to consider each mode equal to the next, I've come to realize the special place of

Mindfulness in our brain, in our personal lives, and in society as a whole. There is something that is transcendent about consciousness. In acknowledging, accepting, and allowing, we are able to create space around our pain-bodied reactions.

Now when I promote Yellow(Mind) to the status of Master Mode, I by no means suggest that it can exist without the other two dimensions. I am only saying that it is sometimes the key to unlock the possibility of +Blue and +Red. I often coach people who are uncertain where to go when Working their Triangle, to "move away" into +Yellow. If there is any doubt about where to go in the Interpersonal Triangle, *go Scarecrow.*

With this in mind, let's talk about Heart. It might be tempting to argue that if any dimension can be called the Master Mode for curing all the ills humanity faces, it would be the Blue(Heart) dimension and love. I do believe (and hope) that eventually love conquers hate. However, I suggest that in order to do true +Blue we often need to go first through +Yellow in order to transcend to the place where we can love well. The royal road from fear and hate to love is often through mindfulness. Think of great people who have changed the course of history (for instance, Buddha, Jesus, Gandhi, and Martin Luther King Jr.). It was necessary for each to first raise their level of awareness and consciousness above and beyond the "conventional wisdom" of their time. They had to contain their own impulses for retaliation and hate. It was only then that love could overcome hate. And this leads us to Yellow's contribution to society.

The Place of Yellow in Society
Scientific Function

There is no creature on earth that knows as much as we do about so many things. I would attribute this to our ability to move away, objectively observe, and experiment—along with a relatively large cerebral cortex. This is what I would call our "scientific function." Together with our +Red ability to compete (and thus improve and evolve), and our +Blue ability to cooperate (work together for common goals and causes), Yellow(Mind) makes a final and major contribution to society's progress—the ability for us to learn and know. Our scientific function together with competition and cooperation (for better or for worse) has yielded complex societies, intricate infrastructures (complete with indoor plumbing), stable and diverse governments, assorted ideologies and religions, numerous fields of study (like psychology, biology, or math), vast amounts of knowledge regarding just about everything imaginable, and let's not forget about all the tools we've made for our use (hammers, super-computers, cell phones, medical equipment, airplanes, and nuclear weapons). Other animals compete and cooperate, but there are none that are nearly as scientific.

As much as we have formal, highly trained scientists by profession, we are all scientists in our own right. We all step back—on occasion—and think about how things work, why things work, and how to make them better. We all conduct our own experiments and wonder what difference it might make if we changed one variable. For instance, if we say something nice to an employee, what difference might it make to their productivity and attitude at work? As "everyday scientists" we also measure things, count things, take data, and take (and fake) statistics. This Yellow(Mind) scientific function has made society what it is today in terms of physical advances. But does it contribute anything to society's morality?

The Morality of Yellow

You wouldn't think that something as neutral as Yellow(Mind) would have any moral relevance to society. Think again. Here are just a few moral ramifications.

Wisdom and Intuition

Knowing that the square root of 36 is 6 is not wisdom; it is knowledge. Knowing what to say (or not say) to a person who just lost their spouse to cancer is wisdom. There are few things that are more valuable than wisdom.

Rules and knowledge are good for those occasions when things are simple and predictable. If your TV is not working, a good rule of thumb is to first determine whether it is plugged in. However, all too often the world is neither simple nor predictable. More often than not, it is complex. And because of this, not every solution fits every situation every time in the same way. But wisdom can discern! Wisdom knows what to do and what to say in the very moment it needs to be done or said.

Wisdom's real-time sound judgment is based on *learning from experience.* Not everyone learns from experience. How many times do we find ourselves doing or saying (or not doing or not saying) the same thing, the same way, with the same (bad) results? When that happens, we have obviously not learned from experience. And that is unfortunate because there is no better teacher. However, when experience is carefully heeded over time, the learning becomes implicit—that is, it becomes a natural part of us. And when this happens, wisdom is born. Along with this implicit wisdom comes good judgment in most any situation and most any context. And this, my friend, is invaluable—to those who are wise, as well as to the societies in which they live. In his best-selling book *Blink,* Malcolm Gladwell talks about the human capacity to make accurate "snap judgments." He calls it "thin-slicing," using limited information to come to an accurate conclusion in a very short time. It is how we think without thinking. It is about following our intuition or "blink" and being right most of the time. He refers to it as the "adaptive unconscious," where we learn from experience based on focusing on accurate or true input. And when this is done well over time it eventually becomes automatic, part of our unconscious. Gladwell describes how an art procurer who had decades of experience with art from antiquity knew in an instant that a recently purchased piece of art by a major museum was a fake. He just *knew.* However, he warns that making decisions when emotionally aroused or when our judgments are based on faulty ideas or biases (emo-tion–notions or narratives), or when we focus on the wrong data points (such as whether a politician is good looking rather than competent), can lead to faulty snap judgments.

In an emotional reaction to 9/11, most politicians in Washington rushed to invade Iraq. They misunder-stood the data and rushed into a war that yielded nu-merous "unintended consequences." It was a mistake that destabilized the entire Middle East, took thou-sands of human lives, cost billions of dollars that we could have spent otherwise, and has created an on-going crisis that still exists at the time of this writing. There were only a few people who ended up having the good judgment—the wisdom—to oppose the war. If only we had listened to them. This raises an impor-tant question. Who should we be listening to now?

Self-Control and Stability

Yellow(Mind) is the stabilizer. It is the keel on the boat in the sea of our emotions. A keel of a boat goes deep enough into the ocean to stabilize the boat when currents and waves would otherwise make the going rough. This is what Yellow(Mind) does for the crash-ing waves of –Blue and/or –Red. It is the part of us that thinks before we (re)act. Where Red(Power) and Blue(Heart) are predominately at home in the limbic system, it seems that Yellow(Mind) resides chiefly in the prefrontal cortex.

In Chapter 5 I quoted Daniel Siegel, one of the co-founders in the field of interpersonal neurobiology. In an April 2006 article for the *Psychiatric Annals,* Siegel wrote the following (I recommend reading it slowly):[4]

> An interpersonal neurobiology view of well-being holds that the complex, nonlinear system of the mind achieves states of self-organization by balancing the two opposing processes of differentiation and linkage. When separated areas of the brain are allowed to specialize in their function and then become linked together, the system is integrated. Integration brings with it a special state or functioning of the whole, which has the acronym of FACES: Flexible, Adaptive, Coherent, Energized and Stable. This coherent flow is bounded on one side by chaos and on the other by rigidity. In this manner we can envision a flow or river of well-being, with the two banks being chaos on the one side, rigidity on the other.

The focal point in this quote is on the idea of a "complex non-linear mind" that is "integrated." Integration comes about when the special differentiated (divergent) functions of the brain are also connected and communicative through linkage (convergence) with each other. As a result we get FACES. If this does not happen we get chaos on one side and/or rigidity on the other. As we consider these five functions of an integrated mind, think of a leader, partner, parent, or friend who has all these functions working together in an integrated way:

   ⅄ Flexible—the ability to bend without breaking.

⅄ Adaptive—ability to adjust to different
conditions.

⅄ Coherent—clear, logical, and forming a whole.

⅄ Energized—having vitality and enthusiasm.

⅄ Stable—firmly established, not easily upset,
not likely to give way.

This is how Siegel describes a mentally healthy
mind. It is a mind that "flows" optimally in a balance
between chaos (disorganization) on one side and rigidity (over-organization) on the other. What I find compelling is that these five integrated brain–mind functions (FACES) aptly describe an emotionally intelligent
person. Emotionally intelligent people are flexible,
adaptive, coherent, energetic, and stable. Emotionally
intelligent people apparently have healthy, integrated
minds.

Who would not like to be married to (or have as
a parent, friend, or boss who is) a person who is flexible, adaptive, coherent, energetic yet stable? On the
other hand, who wants to relate to a spouse (parent,
friend, or boss) who possesses the opposite attributes
of being inflexible or rigid, unable to adapt, incoherent
(confused, unclear, and illogical), depressed, unmoti-
vated, or unstable? Having someone like this in your
life would be at best unpleasant and at worst destructive. And what if that person happens to be you?

This brings up an important question: Can we re-
train the brain? Fortunately, the answer is yes, but it is
a qualified yes. Though everyone is capable of retraining his or her brain to some extent, not everyone is

willing to do what it takes to increase *integration*. Siegel and other neurobiologists agree that in this respect, the brain is "elastic." What they mean by that is that, although difficult, we can recondition the brain—promote new and better mind integration. How does one do this?

The better question at first is "Where do we do this?" There are many brain systems involved, of course, depending on what we are integrating. But one area stands out as it pertains to mind integration: the middle prefrontal cortex. This structure lies at the crossroads between the emotional limbic system and the cerebral cortex (responsible for thinking, language, and other "higher order" functions) and it has to do with regulating activity in other systems so we can experience emotional balance, empathy, insight, fear extinction, intuition, and morality. What neurobiologists have found, interestingly enough, is that a key to developing this part of the brain is through *awareness*. As it turns out, when we raise people's awareness we increase the proper functioning of this important region of the brain, and other regions as a result. If we live a life of awareness we rewire the brain so that the FACES functioning become a natural part of who we are. And the social importance of that makes all the difference in our lives and the world.

Calm and Stillness

Another positive attribute of Yellow(Mind) is a sense of calm, or peace. People who are conscious, aware, and observant are often "chill," mellow Yellow.

The calm space in the +Yellow dimension is a place of stillness. And in my book (literally and figuratively), stillness is good.

Most religions are keen on what distinguishes them (where they diverge) from other religions. But perhaps one of the more subtle aspects of all true spirituality is that of stillness. It is in the stillness we find God. Even if we are atheist or agnostic, we pursue a quest for stillness; a place of serenity. This space is calming and reassuring, but often it is also a place of clarity and creativity. I don't know about you, but so often I think better after a restful break: an interval of stillness. And this place abides in the dimension of Yellow(Mind).

Random-Access Memory (RAM)

Before we leave this section, I want to share one analogy that I am very fond of regarding the mind. I liken the mind to RAM; not the four-legged animal but rather random-access memory. RAM is the place in a computer where the operating system, applications, and data in current use are kept so that they can quickly be reached by the computer. I am old enough to remember the first personal computers. They had very little RAM. If the computer ran much more than two applications at a time, for any length of time, the computer would start to run slowly, get very cranky, and all too often would freeze up and crash. However, even as I am typing this paragraph on my laptop, I have nine applications open on my computer with a much bigger operating system and notably larger applications running and I hardly notice a difference in my laptop's performance. This is because I have a lot of RAM in my computer. But the question that I am asking us here is: Do we have enough RAM—Readily Aware Mindfulness—available to our minds? The more brain RAM we have, the more complexity and ambiguity we can deal with at one time. The more RAM that we have, the more emotions we can feel at one time. People who have a lot of RAM are Flexible, Adaptive, Coherent, Energetic yet Stable (FACES).

However, we all know people who have very little RAM. They cannot deal with complex emotional situations; they cannot handle many feelings—especially painful feelings—before they start to run slowly, get very cranky, and freeze up or even crash. The less RAM we have, the less Flexible, Adaptive, Coherent, and Energetic yet Stable (FACES) we are.

RAM is another way to describe high-quality +Yellow and the more we have of it, the more emotionally intelligent we turn out to be. RAM is spaciousness and the more we have of it the more peaceful, calm, and still we are. This is not only true for individuals but it is true for groups, organizations, and nations as well. Organizational cultures that have very little RAM are typically inflexible. All too often they solve problems in unhealthy ways. For example, Congress at the time of this writing has very little RAM. They are unable to create enough space to work together in spite of opposing views. Terrorist groups have almost no RAM. And because of that, their −Red is violent, and any +Blue compassion and +Yellow self-control and consciousness is missing. On the other hand, organizations, groups, and nations who have a lot of RAM have cultures that are Flexible, Adaptive, Coherent, and Energetic yet Stable (FACES). And this is good for everyone.

Yellow Reactions

In Chapter 1 we discussed the notable problem of human reactivity. Our tendency toward reactivity is the instigator of numerous forms of suffering. It was in Chapter 1 that we introduced Eckhart Tolle's idea of pain-body. If you remember, the pain-body is the accumulated, un-integrated, and coagulated pain that we've experienced earlier in life that was never dealt with (metabolized) and that we can readily re-experience as painful emotion when triggered. It is the part of our psyche that gets inflamed when we are reactive, often in concert with our emotion–notions (narratives) and our Ego being offended. But how does the pain-body vibrate in the –Yellow dimension? How does the Ego defend itself using –Yellow tactics?

Disassociation is a well-known Yellow(Mind) defense employed by people who are not able to escape, so instead they detach within themselves. They emotionally, and even cogitatively, check out. They go offline. The key way that the Ego protects itself in the –Yellow dimension is by disconnection. In essence, we react by not reacting. But when is this healthy self-control (Yellow+) and when is it unhealthy (below-the-line –Yellow) reactivity? This is not always easy to discern.

We all have different thresholds for the amount of pain we can endure before we no longer have enough RAM to process all the input before the human processor crashes. Here are a few other ways that we tend to react in the Yellow(Mind) dimension:

Avoidance

A couple clicks shy of out-and-out disassociation is avoidance. This is where someone anticipates an emotional overload or a challenging relational encounter and deals with it by not dealing with it. One will either brake or circumvent the issue or emotion. I worked with an otherwise-skillful CEO who, when faced with interpersonal challenges, would literally hide in his office and refuse to deal with them—sometimes for years. The results of this avoidance could be measured in millions of dollars in lost revenue and the creation of a defeated and discouraged work culture.

Intellectualization

Some people "think" instead of feel. They do not experience real and powerful emotion (if they can help it) but instead process emotional issues by retreating into their own heads. Don't get me wrong; there is a place for rational and/or analytical understanding and problem-solving. However, intellectualization is not that at all. It is an automatic, unconscious Egoic tactic to avoid real feelings. And let's remind ourselves that God or Evolution did not make a mistake when inventing emotion. Emotions have a vital purpose in the human experience.

Indifference

Some people just don't give a damn about anything or anybody else. As long as it does not affect them, they position themselves in life in a passive, disinterested way. This Egoic defense is not to be confused with the healthy +Yellow position in which things are not taken personally. In their indifference they are uncaring (not +Blue) and non-assertive (not +Red). They go offline. In fact, this Egoic defense might be one of the more subtle forms of selfishness that a human being can exhibit.

Asocial Tendencies

Some pain-bodied people are not good with other people. They are afraid of others and are especially afraid of intimacy and personal need (+Blue). They often keep to themselves or engage only in "safe" social events like computer games or watching sports. Otherwise, they avoid deeper human connection. This is not to be confused with normal introversion. People who fall closer to the introverted end of the extraversion continuum can relate fully with others but not at the same rate of frequency as people with higher levels of extroversion. We vary in how much intentional solitude we prefer, but we all have the need for it at times. This is healthy Yellow(Mind). The unhealthier version of this is an avoidance and even dislike of social encounters or the lack of any sense of need for human connection.

What if You Are a Yellow Reactor?

What if you have a tendency to react in –Yellow? Do you often feel detached or emotionally, psychologically, and relationally cut off? What if you find yourself too often in the below-the-line –Yellow portion of the Relationship Circle? Perhaps you catch yourself avoiding psychological or relationship challenges—of the kind that would have long-term consequences if left unaddressed. If this is you, then you are reading the wrong chapter. If you remember from Chapter 3, the key focus of Working the Triangle is not on what you are doing that is negative (in this case –Yellow), but on what you are not doing that is positive! If you react in Yellow, you would be best served to integrate some +Red and/or +Blue attitudes and behaviors into your repertoire. In light of that, I recommend that you take a look at the relevant parts of the Red(Power) and Blue(Heart) chapters. And I recommend that you consider the Red(Power) chapter, if you react in –Green (–Yellow and –Blue). And I strongly recommend the Blue(Heart) chapter, if you react in –Orange (–Yellow and –Red). See you there.

Working the Triangle: Yellow

The thesis of this book suggests that it is not about what we are doing that is unhealthy or wrong but what we are not doing that is healthy and "right." In light of this chapter, what are the effective ways to respond in +Yellow? This is an important question to answer when we are attempting to Work the Triangle. One way to explore this is to understand what the basic fears are that we tie to the Yellow(Mind) dimension that keeps us from incorporating +Yellow behaviors into our relational repertoire.

Ontological Fear or Anxiety

Ontological fears, as we've stated in previous chapters, are those related to or based upon being or existence. If you recall, the ontological fear associated with Red(Power) is the anxiety related to being "bad" and thus rejected from the tribe. The ontological fear associated with Blue(Heart) is the fear of being weak or vulnerable *within* the tribe. The ontological fear associated with Yellow(Mind) is the fear of being marginalized, if not cut, from the tribe. It is the fear of being insignificant, unimportant, and disenfranchised. It is the fear of being alone!

We mentioned earlier in the chapter that Scarecrow did not feel pain or desire, and had only one fear: the fear of fire. Fire annihilates. It makes something that exists not exist anymore. If we want to get rid of something, we set it on fire and burn it up until there is nothing left but ashes. The ontological fear associated with Scarecrow Yellow(Mind) is the fear of annihilation and nothingness. We are afraid that we will disappear into ashes.

People who are afraid to take a step back into mindfulness often compensate by being super engaged and overly involved (–Purple). They are known to talk too much, and they often ramble. They are afraid that if they stop talking, no one will hear them anymore. They demand a lot of attention lest they should be forced to encounter feelings of insignificance.

There is a scene in the book version of *The Wonderful Wizard of Oz* where the Yellow Brick Road came to an abrupt stop at a river's edge. Across the river Dorothy and her companions could see where the Yellow Brick Road continued on toward the Emerald City. But how would they get across? The Scarecrow (of course) came up with the idea of building a raft. The Tin Man, with a great deal of passion, began to chop down trees with his ax as the Lion competently went to work building the raft. While on the river, the Scarecrow used a pole both to steer and propel the raft across the river. At one fateful point he put the pole into some thick mud, where it quickly became stuck. Because the Scarecrow held on tight, he was immediately pulled from the boat where the rest of the team remained, and was left stranded alone, holding on to the pole in the midst of the river. This vividly portrays the ontological fear associated with Yellow(Mind)—that of being left stranded all alone, abandoned, and separated from the tribe.

Confounded in the Key of Yellow

We already talked about many attitudes and behaviors related to Yellow(Mind) earlier in the chapter. In the same way that people who have fears around Red(Power) and Blue(Heart), people who have fears tied to Yellow(Mind) can easily become confounded. They cannot emotionally tell the difference between healthy detachment (conscious awareness) and unhealthy detachment. Remember the CEO I worked with, Miguel, from Chapter 3? He believed that all Yellow (Mind) was a form of disengagement, which made him "unimportant" in his own mind and insufferably –Purple with everyone else he worked with. Here are a few additional tools and practices that can help you face your Yellow(Mind) fears and create space around what bugs you:

"Take a Breath"

If there is one thing that you can do to bring you immediately into a healthy Yellow(Mind) state it would be to take some deep breaths. Take note of your breathing next time you are stressed. It is likely shallow and tight, and highly ineffective in getting necessary oxygen into your body. However, taking a series of deep breaths (from your diaphragm—not your upper chest) when you are in a reactive state has a way of centering and calming. It helps to produce mellow +Yellow.

Deep breathing moves us from the sympathetic nervous system state to the parasympathetic nervous system state—the relaxed and calm nervous system. So if you are reacting in any of the three dimensions, and you are fortunate enough to become aware of it while it is happening, one way to stop it in its tracks is to take half a dozen deep diaphragm breaths. You will notice the difference immediately.

Meditation

It would be negligent to have a chapter on Yellow(Mind) without mentioning meditation. Meditation means many things to many people. For some it is a weird, if not forbidden, Eastern religious practice. For many it is a form of prayer, for others it is guided imagery, and for still others it is a practice for stilling the mind.

Almost all spiritual disciplines use techniques that resemble meditation in one form or another; human beings have practiced it for thousands of years. With the new technologies that allow for brain imaging, we now know why. Two forms of meditation that have been extensively studied include mindfulness meditation and something called "compassion meditation." Both of these forms are known to bring about measureable changes in brain matter as well as in cortisol levels. And considering what we've learned about the effects of prolonged, high levels of cortisol, many of the benefits of meditation will not surprise you.

When you have a free day with nothing to do, I invite you to Google the phrase "benefits of meditation." It will take you that long to read about all the known benefits of this ancient practice.[5] Here are just a few: Meditation slows aging in the brain, preserving more gray matter; reduces mind wandering and rumination—both of which can lead to depression; improves concentration, along with other cognitive skills; decreases anxiety; increases compassion for others; and increases self-control, thereby helping us fight addictions. Meditation also boosts the immune system, lowers blood pressure, and improves breathing and heart rates.

Many of us exercise on a daily basis. We run, lift weights, swim, or take brisk walks in order to strengthen our muscles and our cardiovascular system (and to drop a few pounds). If we want to strengthen our prefrontal cortex and the Yellow(Mind) dimension, we should meditate on a regular basis as well. We build physical strength with exercise; we build mental strength—Yellow(Mind)—with meditation.

I personally find meditation difficult. My mind wanders. I have a hard time sitting still for very long. But here is the good news: The act of returning to a calm state helps to build the prefrontal cortex. So every time we catch our mind wandering while we try to meditate and we gently bring our mind back to a meditative state, we are strengthening our prefrontal cortex. And in doing so we strengthen Scarecrow's rule in our internal Emerald City. That is a good thing.

Chapter 7

Synergy and Finding Balance in All Our Relationships

Unus pro omnibus, omnes pro uno
("One for all, all for one").
The motto of *The Three Musketeers,*
by Alexandre Dumas

It was wrong what I did. In the previous three chapters, I did something unnatural. I tore reality apart. It's impossible to talk about Red(Power), Blue(Heart), and Yellow(Mind) independently of one another. They can only be truly understood in context. And positive change can only happen with the constructive balance in each dimension. You can no more consider Heart from Power from Mind than you can take the literal human heart, the skeletal-muscular system, from the brain. They exist together. They either work together or they work against each other, but they in real life they cannot be separated.

In Chapter 4, I invited the reader to imagine a world without Red(Power). At first it sounds great: a world where there is no fighting or hatred. Where people do not attack, malign, envy, or hate. But imagination can take us only so far until we realize this world without Red(Power) would be a world lacking any distinctiveness and diversity. A world full of only Green(Peace) (Yellow + Blue) would also be a world of passivity. There would be no progress, no assertiveness, no effort, no fighting for justice. The fact is that we have no choice; there is no world without Red(Power). The only choice that we have is to incorporate +Blue and +Yellow to make the Red(Power) of high quality.

And there is no world without Blue(Heart). Can you imagine a heartless world, a world without love or care or regard for others? Can you picture a world without cooperation or collaboration and teamwork? It would be a world full of sociopaths. Sociopaths have a relative incapacity for empathy and true care for others. For the most part, they do things out of selfish expediency. What would a world full of sociopaths look like? It would be a world of exploitation and mutual deprivation and destruction.

And there can be no world, as we know it, without Yellow(Mind). There would be only animalistic urges without regard for rule of law and "truth." It would be a society dominated by immediate impulses. There would be no self-control. Sigmund Freud introduced us to the idea of the "id." The id is the part of the mind in which innate instinctive impulses and primary processes are manifest. Without Yellow(Mind) these primary processes would be the only process and would generate a world of utter mayhem.

The integrity to our emotional life lies in the fact that we exist in a world made up of three relational dimensions. And we cannot understand our emotional or relational life apart from the three dimensions taken together. (It is for this reason that I use a triangle to indicate the interconnectedness of the three dimensions.) Take, for example, the important issue discussed in the previous three chapters of convergence, divergence, and observance. All human beings are connected to each other (biologically and energetically) and yet at the same time we are distinct from one another based on numerous variables (intelligence, personality, race, gender, political affiliation, religion, and culture). And last, but not least, we observe the tension between convergence and divergence. The Yellow(Mind) dimension allows us to tolerate the apparent contradiction between convergence and divergence so we can respect each other's differences without prejudice, while at the same time recognizing all that makes us "one" without losing our uniqueness.

As we noted in Chapter 2, if even one of the dimensions is avoided out of fear, Ego, or habit, the other dimensions will go out of balance and manifest negative (below-the-line) low-quality attitudes and relational behaviors. This is what happens when we become reactive. We are thrown out of balance. That's the bad news. Here's the good news: When we integrate the positive aspects of all three dimensions in our responses to others and the world, we function in that moment at a transcendent level.

Fully human, fully alive people are fully engaged in all the three dimensions in a positive, dynamic, and integrated (synergistic) way. Each positive aspect of one dimension augments the other two aspects until we can relate at the pinnacle of the Interpersonal Triangle. We manifest and experience fullness and flow in the optimal energy field. This is peak human functioning—whether it is a spouse with his partner, a parent with a child, a leader with her executive team, an organizational culture with its employees, or a government with its people. The goal of this book is to help people and organizations grow in the direction of this lofty human ideal—finding the balance of power, heart, and mindfulness in all our relationships.

This describes what we have called in this book the human sweet spot: the psychological place where we live most dynamically with the least amount of energy expended and the most positive energy generated. We discussed in chapters 2 and 3 the idea that we are all made up of energy. The energy that is emitted from the balanced integrated human being (or group or organization) operating from the sweet spot is positive and contagious. Generally balanced people make other people around them relax and feel positive. Inadvertently they bring out the best in everyone they encounter. This is true for organizations as well. There are endless studies demonstrating that psychologically healthy workplaces produce an environment or "culture" that naturally brings out the best in its people.

One implication of reaching for this sweet spot has to do with changing our inner, family, and corporate narratives. Most of our inner personal narratives about the self and the world we live in are informed, if not distorted, by our pain-body and Ego, conditioned and artificially reinforced over years of faulty learning. How do we change our inner narratives in a way that reflects the positive aspects of all three dimensions? So, for example, how would we change our narrative of "strength" or power to include heart and mindfulness (+Green)? Or how would we embrace a caring for others that includes keeping good boundaries (+Orange)?

This idea of rewriting our narrative applies to groups as well. Any group of any size that exists for any given length of time eventually creates its own narratives. We call this "organizational culture." So can a hard-driving corporate culture include some regard for employee work–life balance? Or could Congress include in its narrative about ideological purity also appropriate negotiation and compromise in order to actually get something done?

There are no individuals, families, or organizations that I know of who live in their sweet spot on a consistent basis. I certainly don't maintain this optimal level of functioning. I'd like to think that maybe there are some people who can fully and constantly live in the high-energy field of the dynamic balance of power, heart, and mindfulness. I just don't know anyone personally like that. Life is too complicated and challenging for most people to hold up and stay engaged in all three (above-the-line) dimensions. But the times that I do operate from the sweet spot are times of great joy and personal fulfillment. Likewise, I do not know of anyone who has approximated this emotional intelligence without conscious effort. Regardless of how healthy their parents were and how good their genetics they still have some sort of pain-body that will derail them to some degree.

All of us either by current anxiety, ego-defensiveness and/or long-term habit get thrown out of balance when one or more the dimensions are avoided. I call this avoided dimension our least-preferred movement (LPM). Even though our LPM often changes depending on the current challenge or situation, many of us will find that we have a particular movement that we avoid. And what we don't realize is that when we avoid our least-preferred movement or dimension, we avoid our chance to transcend to our next level of personal capacity.

This is the very basis of Working the Triangle, which we introduced in Chapter 3. As you recall, Working the Triangle is based on the idea that the critical issue to focus on is not what we are doing that is wrong, but what we are not doing that is right. Working the Triangle is a tool that we can use anytime we are thrown out of balance in a relationship. But it is also something that we can practice on an ongoing basis as individuals, groups, and nations to mature and grow. It is a way to become more emotionally intelligent. It is a way to become a better person, spouse, parent, sibling, friend, leader, organization, or government.

Applications to Real-Life Roles

In this section we turn our attention to seven real-life roles in which we can find ourselves. I picked these particular roles because they are the most familiar to me in my work as a clinician and as an organizational consultant, but also because I believe that most readers will identify with at least one of the roles that we will review. The coverage is not meant to be exhaustive. A complete treatment of each is beyond the scope of this book. Rather, this section will reflect on how the three dimensions and the Interpersonal Triangle might be relevant to these most important roles. I invite you to pick and choose from the following offerings that most apply to you.

Dating and Mating

One of the most important decisions we will ever make in our lives is who we "pair up with," whether for a short time (as in dating) or for our entire life (as in mate selection). This "decision" is profound in its effect on the quality of our lives. There is a reason I put "decision" in quotation marks. You see, we fool ourselves to think that who we are attracted to and/or who we attract is of our own accord and choice. To a large extent our *un-conscious Yenta* pairs us up with others. And the more unconscious we are in this process the more likely we will pick someone who will play a starring role in our pain-body narrative. How is it that the things we thought were so cute when we first started to date become the very things that eventually drive us crazy later? Or we realize—down the road—that he or she is exactly like my (neurotic) mother or my (narcissistic) father. How did we miss that? (Well, *we* might have missed it but our pain-body did not.)

What does this have to do with the three dimensions, you might ask? Everything! Very often what is under-developed in us (our LPM) is the very thing that we attract and are attracted to in the other. Take Glen and Mindy, for example. Glen is quiet by nature and insecure by early life experience. He had a domineering mother and a distant father. His weakest (LPM) dimension is in the Red(Power) dimension. Mindy, on the other hand, is energetic and bold. Her LPM was in the Yellow(Mind) dimension. She had a basic anxiety around not being important. Like two hydrogen molecules and an oxygen molecule, they were attracted to each other immediately. At first, she liked his quiet, peaceful temperament. It was calming to her, and he seemed to enjoy her boisterous (Purple) ways. She knew what she wanted and was not afraid to tell you. Glen, in fact, did love her energy and confidence. She often made decisions for them, which was initially a relief for someone unsure of his own choices. However, later in the relationship he tired of her relentless "energy" and was both annoyed and defeated by her control of him. On the other hand, Mindy was eventually frustrated by Glen's apparent passivity and lack of drive—all too similar to her mother's.

Variations of this story are notably common where the dimension that is underdeveloped in a person is attractive to them—at first—in someone else. And when you get both parties attracted to each other based on what is missing in them at the same time (like Mindy and Glen) you get an irresistible attraction and a formidable albeit invisible bond. This is just basic *relational chemistry.*

This process is never truer than when both parties are relatively unconscious (unaware of themself and the other) and out of balance on the Interpersonal Triangle. This combination is deadly when it comes to many things, not the least of which is dating, and even more so mate selection. There is another way to say this: There is nothing that you can do that is better for you in dating and mate selection than being more aware and conscious of yourself and to be continually Working your Triangle.

I work with a woman who has a "habit" of finding men who are narcissistic, controlling, and detached with little or no empathy (–Orange). In fact, her last husband was a sociopath who threw her under the bus during the divorce process—with the help of a vicious lawyer—leaving her virtually with no money and no way to take care of herself. She is understandably concerned about dating again. She realizes that she keeps attracting the same kind of person—even though they seem "nice" when they are first dating. My advice is to raise her consciousness above her narrative of finding Prince Charming (most narcissists are very charming) and begin working on her own +Orange attributes and behaviors.

There is a rule in family systems that we attract people at the same or similar level of maturity. If you are at a level 6 (with 10 being fully mature and 1 being an emotional wreck), you will likely be interested in and attract another person around 6 (even if they are totally different than you in personality). Daniel Siegel, a leader in the field of interpersonal neurobiology to whom we have referred in earlier chapters, refers to a healthy mind as one that is Flexible, Adaptive, Coherent, Energized, and Stable (FACES). If this is the sort of person you would like to attract—a mature FACES boyfriend/girlfriend or mate—then work at becoming such a person yourself. I have a phrase that I use with couples: *We deserve whom we marry.* So if you consistently attract apparent narcissists you might want to sign up for some psychotherapy and work on your +Orange (+Red and +Yellow). If you attract more passive people, you might want to consider developing your +Yellow dimension. And if you attract a mature, decent, fun person, then be very grateful (and take a bow). And no matter what, keep Working your Triangle. It will improve your dating life.

Marriage and Partnerships

Once we date, we mate. Traditionally, we get married when we mate. More couples these days decide not to legally marry but they still mate. They still identify with each other as some sort of a "relational unit" with shared emotional, psychological, fiscal, and logistic space. In this section, when I use the term *married*, I refer to everyone who are bound together in some sort of ongoing committed relationship. I will also use the term *conjugal* to cover all committed relationships as well. And even as the Interpersonal Triangle applies to us when we are dating it is even more dynamic when we are married.

I often joke "God was in a bad mood when S/he invented marriage." There is no relationship more desired yet more difficult to be in. The greatest proportion of songs written and movies made involve people "falling in love." But what they don't tell you is that once you "fall" it is hard to get up. It was a little easier when we lived with strict rules of engagement. A man took care of his woman financially and she took care of him in every other way, especially in giving him babies. But the 20th century brought with it a gender revolution that shook everything up. This much-needed course correction brings with it a lot of confusion and emotional reactivity, however. Although we no longer follow the previous oppressive rules of yesteryear, we are still trying to figure out how to live together as independent agents without high amounts of reactivity. We have not found the balance of power, heart, and mindfulness in our intimate relationships.

One reason for the notable challenges of being happily married relates to our emotion–notions—our pain-body and Ego. Members of a couple are notably and psychological identified with one another. Because of this, the boundaries between them are very permeable and easily infiltrated with all kind of emotional "stuff." There is relatively little emotional space between the members in a couple. Expectations of having the most basic needs met are high, and the inevitable and frequent failure of this need-meeting is met with deep hurt and offense.

For this reason, the conjugal relationship is a primary feeding ground for the pain-body. In the previous section on dating we talked about the unconscious matching of our emotion notions and pain-body narratives. Well the story grows when we get married. There is probably no other relationship that activates the pain-body and offends and threatens the Ego as much as a conjugal relationship. And with this comes notably reactivity in the poor-quality sectors of all three dimensions.

The Interpersonal Triangle gives us a model to understand this. Remember Glen and Mindy? Well, they got married. (They had no choice. They had to. Their pain-bodies arranged it long before Mindy forced him to propose.) It is difficult to know when and how these things get started, but at some point Mindy was experienced as too controlling. And as much as Glen hated this, he did not know how to adequately communicate this to her. Because he was not versed in +Red, he became passive-aggressive instead. He turned out to be very good at being passive-aggressive—a pro. When Mindy sensed this, she unconsciously turned up the control buttons adding some blame and criticism to make it more intense. This only drove him further away. By then their pain-bodies were both fully inflamed and their Egos duly threatened and offended. (Because this book is rated PG, I cannot go into the details of what happened next. All I can tell you is that it was not pretty.) Since then, they have often found themselves staring into each other's narrative about their painful life. Soon this pattern of relating will become automatic. It will not take much to trigger each other's pain-body now. The only recourse left at their disposal is to build defenses. He may do this by working long hours and watching porn, and she may become preoccupied with the kids—perhaps mixing an extra cocktail at night "just to help her relax."

This is only one of many possible scenarios that can result as couples trigger one another. There are many diverse combinations of ways we might react to each other below the line. It doesn't always look the same. Sometimes one person will habitually "cave in" to the whims and perspectives of the other—taking on the role of the martyr. Often we can start in one dimension (e.g., avoidant –Yellow) but then move into another (e.g., –Red rage or –Blue surrender) out of desperation. But none of these reactions are helpful. While each person's pain-body feasts on the yummy misery and unhappiness, their reactions are effectively destroying the love that once made their relationship fulfilling. And as time goes on without any increased awareness and changes in behavior, it only gets worse. At best people drift apart. At worst the relationship becomes destructive, often leading to divorce and sometimes even worse—emotional and physical abuse.

An entire book could be written on how to apply the Interpersonal Triangle model to intimate relationships. It is enough here to say a few things:

- ⋏ It is difficult, but for most people it is possible to find a new, more empowered, loving, and mindful way to relate. And this comes, of course, by Working the Triangle. If you are reacting –Red (like Mindy), think about more +Blue or +Yellow things you can do or say. If you are reacting –Yellow (like Glen) think of more +Blue and +Red things that can be brought in to how you relate to your partner. And of course if you are –Blue (like Betty in Chapter 3), work on more +Red and +Yellow skills to incorporate into your interaction. It takes time, patience, and a lot of forgiveness. Because of this, look for small changes in yourself and your partner. As the 12-step people say, "progress not perfection."

- ⋏ You might need the help of a professional who can stand in the position of Scarecrow— the Observer—until you can do this more for yourselves.

Even if your relationship has not deteriorated to the point described above, it can always be better. Working the Triangle is not just for couples in dire straits. It can be for anyone who wants a relationship to be better. Each time we achieve a higher, more balanced level of functioning, we get to experience a more dynamic love and agency and the joy that comes with it.

Parenting

And once we mate we procreate. There are at least two aspects of the Interpersonal Triangle that apply to parenting. The first is our reactivity versus responsiveness as parents. The second has to do with helping our children grow into people who are balanced in their personal agency, heart, and mindfulness.

Reactive or Responsive Parenting

Have you ever lost your patience with or nagged one of your children? Have you ever let your child talk you into something that was not good for either you or for them? Have you ever ignored the needs or wants of your child when trying to meet your own? If the answer to all of these questions is "no, never," then you can skip this section—or better yet, you can write this section. Otherwise, this is one more occasion to practice Working the Triangle, this time with your children, regardless of whether they are 6 days old or 60 years old. To illustrate working the Interpersonal Triangle with children, I will once again embarrass both of mine.

When my children were both young, they loved to do fantasy play. My wife was really good at fantasy play with them. She would seamlessly jump into the scene that they created with their doll or action figures and she would join them in their remarkably imagined story. This is a testimony to my wife's +Blue capacities. For me it was an entirely different story. I found fantasy play stressful after a very short time. And because of this I reacted –Yellow. I avoided it like the plague and when cornered by a request that offered no viable exit, I endured with little enthusiasm. If I were to Work the Triangle in this situation, I would have acknowledged and accepted my disability to be child-like (in the best sense of the word) and by doing this I would have created space around my anxiety. This space would then make it more possible for me to find my inner child who could come out and play (+Blue) with my imaginative children. In this case I would have been responsive to my children rather than reactive.

As is the case with almost all adolescents, my daughter would test our boundaries. For her this sometimes took the form of staying out past her assigned curfew. I found myself strangely afraid to confront her. Instead I went –Green where I was overly permissive (–Blue) and avoidant (–Yellow) of her. I remember one night hearing her come in late and just lying in bed pretending to be asleep in order to avoid a confrontation with her. It was clear what I needed to do as a responsible father. The color missing in a –Green reaction is +Red. I needed to acknowledge and accept my fear of confronting her and facing her reaction. If I had done this, it would have created enough space around my anxiety to intentionally access my Courageous Lion by saying something to her.

I present one more example of Working the Triangle, this time regarding my son. My son was one of those kids who was mature beyond his age without being precocious. He is confident and very chill—too chill sometimes for my comfort. I often found myself wishing he was more "worried" about things that he needed to do and more passionate about pursuing those of his interests that I saw as having potential value. In reaction to his Yellow(Mind) disposition, I would (not so) subtly bug him about pursuing his abilities, responsibilities, and interests. In order to prevent myself from reacting to his different pace, I had to Work the Triangle. I needed to respond with more +Yellow. To do this I needed to acknowledge and accept *my* anxiety about *my* inner story about him, and with this acknowledgment allow the space to form around *my* anxiety so that I could move away and let him discover things in his own time. To my great surprise he did end up pursuing his responsibilities and creative interests without me bugging him. Go figure!

So how do you need to Work the Triangle with each of your own children regardless of their age or personality? As you must have noticed in the above examples, I had to practice different dimensions depending on my personal reaction to the situation and their personality. (In the first situation requiring fantasy play, I needed to practice +Blue; in the second, with my daughter, +Red; and in the third example, with my son, +Yellow.)

In all likelihood each child, in each situation, will trigger a different reaction in you. Acknowledging your reaction is the beginning of Working the Triangle. It is all too easy to simply blame our reaction on our demanding young children, a boundary-challenging or "slow-paced" teenager and miss the one thing that we actually have control over—our own reactivity. To do that is to miss the opportunity to transcend our more pain-bodied Ego-driven self to find a balance between power, heart, and mindfulness as a parent.

Building a Transcendent Child

Most parents want their children to have a better life than they have. We want our children to do better in school and work, have more positive experiences, and be more successful in the challenges that they face. So why wouldn't we want our children to be more emotionally intelligent, personally secure, and relationally successful? In essence we would want them to be more conversant, competent, and limber in the three relational and emotional dimensions. We want them to find a dynamic balance between personal agency, heart, and mindfulness. Therefore, we would want to help them Work their Triangle throughout their childhood. So if we find that a child is inclined to be shy in certain situations, how do we (gently) encourage them to be more proactive? If we have a child who tends to be bossy, how do we engender a capacity for inclusion and empathy in their social repertoire?

The Interpersonal Triangle can be a road map to help us identify the places where we want to help our children stretch and grow in order to be more balanced as adults. But a note of caution is warranted here. We have to be careful to wisely navigate somewhere between indifference on one side and anxious control on the other. On the one hand we might never help that shy child ask someone for a play date. Instead, we might always do things for them so that they never develop the Red(Power) capacity for themselves. If we don't help them shore up some necessary relational skills and capacities, we might handicap them for life. But on the other hand, we have to be careful not to be too heavy handed (pun intended). If we become too anxious—like I did with my son—we can communicate the wrong thing to our children. We might suggest that they are not okay the way they are. Once again we need to call on Scarecrow to be our wisdom on how to navigate this parenting challenge.

Our daughter was one of those kids who was generally and easily liked. Because of this she mostly waited for the next suitor for a play date to call. As parents we were concerned that she might rest too much on her laurels, rendering her dependent on others to pursue her. So we gently encouraged her to reach out to kids that she enjoyed and wanted to be friends with. We encouraged her to be more +Red. We helped her Work her Triangle.

I've worked with more than one set of parents who had a child who had too little Yellow. Let's take

4-year-old Marianne as an example. As a result of her difficulty with Yellow(Mind), Marianne had relatively very little tolerance for frustration of any kind. So if her parents put a restriction on her (e.g., time to go home or she had to wait for dessert until after a meal) she would often have a catastrophic temper tantrum, throwing herself on the floor, yelling, screaming, and even at times biting. The first challenge—and a difficult one at that—was to help the parents manage their own reaction to Marianne's temper tantrum. Few things are more disturbing to a parent then when their child goes ballistic, especially in public. So they each had to work their own triangle. The next challenge here was to help Marianne incorporate more +Yellow, both while the temper tantrum was occurring and over time to develop a capacity she could use for the rest of her life. We worked on holding her during a temper tantrum, acknowledging and accepting her upset, and reassuring her that she would be okay. The parents encouraged her to use her words instead. And if necessary they would have Marianne go to a quiet place to "calm down," after which they would talk about what she had felt or wanted. They had to walk the narrow path between being responsive and not being manipulated by her intense and provocative behavior. At the same time, the parents were encouraged to model the calm state they wanted Marianne to eventually have. Don't believe me if I tell you that this was easy for Marianne's parents and that it worked perfectly every time. But over time, some improvements were noted. And as I often like to say, "A little change is a lot."

Now let's turn our attention to the world of work.

Leadership

Have you ever worked for a bad boss? They come in all different shapes and sizes—or should we say colors. There are bad bosses who come from the –Red paint bucket, who are impatient, angry, demeaning, and critical. There are the passive, pushover, indecisive leaders who come from the –Blue bucket and, perhaps the worst of all, the detached leaders who come out of the –Yellow paint bucket. Do you recall from Chapter 3 the study from Kaiser and Kaplan? In an extensive study of hundreds of managers they identified four types of managers. Here are the four types again:

⋏ The Lopsided Forceful manager, from our –Red dimension.

⋏ The Lopsided Enabling manager straight out of our –Blue dimension.

⋏ The Disengaged manager, who was voted the least effective from the –Yellow dimension.

⋏ The Versatile manager, who had just the right amount +Red and +Blue with enough +Yellow to know which to use and when. This leader was significantly more effective than any of the other three. This is our synergistic leader; it is our emotionally intelligent leader.

This is the leader we all would want for a boss. This is the leader that we want to lead our work teams, our companies, and our government. This is the leader we should aspire to be.

There are numerous studies—too many to mention here—that consistently find that leaders with high emotional intelligence (EQ) are, for the most part, better leaders. The opposite is of course true as well. Lower EQ is correlated with less-effective employees, managers, and leaders. Anyone who has ever worked for either a very good leader or very bad leader already knows this.

I want to mention that my view of leadership as I use it here is broad. I am not just talking about the CEO of a company. I am talking about line managers, sales reps, and teachers in the classroom. A janitor at a high school can be a leader in his or her own right. A leader is anyone who takes it upon himself or herself to influence the behaviors of others for the good of that person and/or the organization or group for which they participate.

Leaders and managers who have high-quality EQ bring out the best in other people. In Chapter 2 we talked about the positive energy that people have when they live above the line in the Relationship Circle. This positive energy is contagious. In Chapter 1 we refer to the book *Primal Leadership*.[1] In this book, Goleman and his colleagues talk about "resonant leadership." Resonant leaders, just by virtue of their dynamic balance, naturally and unconsciously effect and affect people around them for good. The positive energy from their limbic system resonates with the limbic systems of their employees. By doing this they create good feelings and a positive work environment.

So how do we get these people into our organizations, nonprofits, boardrooms, religious institutions, institutions of education, and Congress? The best way to get balanced, high EQ leaders is to select them (and elect them for Congress). I often tell corporate clients that it is easier to hire a person with high EQ than it is to train a person to develop a higher EQ. That is why a good amount of my corporate consulting involves helping companies in the hiring process.[2] And as much as that is a very good idea, it is not easy to detect and determine highly EQ people in the interview process— when people are on their best behavior and narcissists turn on their charm. It is not much easier to detect emotional intelligence with psychological testing, either, which is reliant on the self-report of the candidate. But you have a fighting chance to beat the odds if you are least vetting for emotional intelligence in the interview process (along with the necessary skills and experience). So it behooves people involved in the selection process to look for positive attributes in all three dimensions:

> ⅄ +Red attributes of agency, decisiveness, ability to confront others, to speak one's mind; to be assertive, appropriately aggressive, and competitive. One needs to be willing to fight for the organization.

> ⅄ +Blue attributes of emotional connectedness, empathy, good listening skills, and a genuine care for other people. I often suggest that companies take final candidates out for dinner and see how they relate to the waiter or waitress.

⮥ +Yellow attributes of self-control, anger, and anxiety management; ability to consider and contain contradictory and intense emotions as well as withstand the reactivity of other people.

The more common way to have emotionally intelligent people in organizations is through training, coaching, and mentoring programs for already existing employees and leaders. And this is where the Interpersonal Triangle comes in. It is not difficult to determine from interviews, some psychological testing, and multi-rater assessments,[3] the LPM of most leaders in any given context. This type of training, coaching, and/or mentoring is not only for executives who are ready to fall off the rails. In fact, they are most useful for employees who show promise—what we call HiPo, or high-potential employees. These programs are also useful for people who have been promoted into a position that presents new challenges.

Work Teams

Most organizations no longer are led by a single authoritarian leader. More and more organizations are being led by teams of people (who are led perhaps by a single leader). Why? Organizations are being led by teams because no one person has all the attributes necessary to run a complex business in an ever-changing complex marketplace. These executive-level leadership teams are of course not the only teams who have an impact on an organization. Teams are also extensively used in organizations to work on projects together. And they do this for the same reason—diversity of necessary skills and abilities. In Chapter 5, I introduced you to the work of Meredith Belbin. Based on his extensive research on work teams, he proposed nine roles that need to be in play in order for a team to be successful, and no one person has all nine attributes. In other words, human beings are team-oriented. Since the beginning of human history we hunted together and we parented children together and we fought together—as a team.

There's one major problem with teams. Unfortunately, they are made up of people. If it were not for people who have pain-bodies and Egos, teams would work well most of the time. In fact, when a team works together it is a lovely thing to behold. However, when a team falls apart, especially due to emotional reactivity, it is not only ugly it is downright destructive to the purpose of the team and the organization it "supports." This is where the Interpersonal Triangle comes in again. Anytime there is emotional reactivity, Working the Triangle is the road map to getting people back on track.

Here are few places where people in a team can get into each other's way:

–Red Attitudes and Behaviors

It only takes one or two people in a team with unchecked –Red attitudes and behaviors to ruin the effectiveness of a team. You only need one bully or overly domineering person to demoralize the rest of the team. You only need one person who is competitive within the team, jockeying for positions of power and notoriety, to spoil the teamwork.

–Blue Attitudes and Behaviors

If you have too many –Blue people in a group, you end up with something called *groupthink*. Groupthink is a phenomenon when everyone gets locked into thinking the same way as everyone else. You might say, what's wrong with people agreeing? Everything is wrong if all the options and perspectives are not considered first. One of the benefits of working in a team is the diversity of opinions and perspectives. If there is no one in the group who can think critically many projects will run into unanticipated problems or are doomed to go over budget.

–Yellow Attitudes and Behavior

This is the deadly detachment and indifference of the poor-quality –Yellow. I remember working with an executive team who was dealing with a complex challenge. The major stakeholder in the group remained silent over a prolonged period of time as the rest of the team struggled. Finally, the executive, after a long time of seeming indifference, finally spoke up only after being asked. He had the solution the whole time but didn't care to say it. As a result, many opportunities and revenue were loss.

What difference might it make if you had a team of engaged team members with diverse skills and perspectives (a-la Belbin) along with high emotional intelligence and balance so that they communicated well and with respect? That is the winning combination: diversity of skill and high EQ. It would make all the difference in the world. Why? Because the whole team would be energetically above the line.

- ▲ +Red. People would be free to speak their minds and raise their concerns—not caught up in groupthink. People would freely challenge each other.

- ▲ +Blue. They would challenge each other but with the utmost empathy and respect. They would challenge the ideas but not the person. They would all be good listeners, and they would care about the good of the group and the organization rather than themselves.

- ▲ +Yellow. People would be thoughtful, reflecting, and exhibiting self-control when interacting with their teammates. They would acknowledge and accept being upset and in doing so, would create space around their feelings. They would not take things personally. Instead, they would be mindful and conscious.

When I work with work groups I often give them a personality test (like the DiSC, the SDI, or my

Interpersonal Triangle Inventory) so that they can see where they need to focus their attention in order to become a more emotionally intelligent team member. And when everyone does this in a concerted effort, the performance of the group improves dramatically.

Organizational Culture

Organizational culture is the "personality" of the organization. Culture consists of the prevalent values, beliefs, and attitudes that characterize a company and directs its behavior. To some extent, a company's internal culture may be articulated in its mission statement or vision statement.[4] But in many ways, a culture goes beyond what a company can say about itself in the same way that we as individuals are so much more than we can personally describe about ourselves. In this sense, a company has an "unconscious" or at least a "subconscious." In other words, there are implicit aspects of an organizational culture that are as hard to immediately discern in the same way that the unconscious of an individual is not readily apparent. But these implicit aspects of a culture are at least as dynamic as the conscious aspects of the culture—if not more so.

I belong to a company that specializes in organizational culture, and one of the first challenges we face as consultants is discerning how to help our client organization understand itself. We assess the *explicit* part of their culture by reviewing their mission statements, policies, and practices. We also give standardized assessments that measure organizational culture.[5] Getting at the implicit aspects of a culture is more interesting and a lot more challenging. We assess the implicit aspects of the culture indirectly by conducting interviews with individuals and groups. We ask them to tell us stories about the company and "how they really do things around here." We then analyze and synthesize what we find into hypotheses (or educated guesses) about the full culture of the company, especially as it pertains to the challenges that they face. Here are just a few issues we examine:

- ▲ How does their culture align with their strategy, and how is it at cross-purposes to their stated strategy?

- ▲ How does the culture reflect the positive or negative attitudes, values, and behaviors of its leaders?

- ▲ Does the organizational culture enhance or degrade the effectiveness and productivity of an organization?

- ▲ What if the company is acquiring (or merging with) another company? How will their companies "converge," anticipating possible things that could go wrong?

▲ How does culture help or degrade the relationships within an organization (happy or unhappy employees) and outside the organization (happy or unhappy clients and customers)?

This raises a question: If individuals can be emotionally intelligent (or not), can organizations be emotionally intelligent (or not)? I would, of course, suggest yes. And the Interpersonal Triangle model can inform us on what an emotionally intelligent organization would look like. Please see Table 7.1 to see some potential characteristics of healthy organizational cultures.

Quality --> Dimension:	Positive, High-Quality Culture That...	Negative, Low-Quality Culture That...
Red(Power)	• Tells the truth to others regardless of rank • Is hard-driving and competitive • Expects the best from its employees and leaders • Is not afraid to fire low EQ or poor performers	• Uses intimidation and fear to motivate its employees • Punishes more than it rewards • Fires people without cause or for political reasons
	And	Or
Blue(Heart)	• Advocates and models cooperation and collaboration • Values and cherishes all employees who truly contribute • Invests resources in the development of its people • Listens and values input from all employees • Will give people a chance to prove themselves before they fire them	• Lets people "get by" with low or inferior job performance • Is intimidated by employees, vendors, or clients • Gives too much to clients or customers without regard for real business realities
	And	Or
Yellow(Mind)	• Has a clear and realistic strategy for both its culture and its success • Makes decisions thoughtfully, based on facts and data • Generates a practice of self-control and measured responses • Advocates thinking before acting	• Has a "hands-off" mentality about solving problems • Practices "conflict avoidance" • Overly analytical and "safe"; will not take risks

Table 7.1: Healthy Versus Unhealthy Organizational Cultures

Conclusion

If you have read this far into the book, there is not much more for me to pass along. The person that we are meant to be, our "best-self," is already inside us; we just have to release that person. My humble contribution to this endeavor is to suggest the practice of Working the Triangle. We do this in order to transcend our old emotion–notions, pain-body, and Ego-driven reactivity, which suppresses and represses our truest and best self. The goal, instead, is to release our best and most positive energies—not far in the future but every time we find the dynamic balance of personal Power, Heart, and Mindfulness. "Godspeed!"

Notes

Chapter 1

1. Tolle first uses the term *pain-body* in his book, *The Power of Now*.

2. Carl Jung talked about something similar when he talked about the Shadow archetype.

3. Sam Alibrando, *Follow the Yellow Brick Road: How to Change for the Better When Life Gives You Its Worst* (Bloomington, IN: iUniverse, 2007).

4. Source: http://www.detoxifynow.com/et_pain_body.html. Whether you believe in his spiritual

or energetic explanation, I find his description of pain-body compelling based on hundreds of business and clinical clients that I have worked with over the years.

5. The term *daemon* (Latin), used to describe a dangerous or evil spirit, came into use via Plato and his pupil Xenocrates. The Greek *daimon* is the form used in the New Testament's original text, and this was used to describe the Judeo-Christian concept of an evil spirit by about the second century AD. Anthony Grafton, Glenn W. Most, and Salvatore Settis, *The Classical Tradition* (Cambridge, MA: Belknap, 2010), 260.

6. Jonathan Haidt, *The Happiness Hypothesis* (Cambridge: Perseus, 2006).

7. Malcolm Gladwell, *Blink: The Power of Thinking Without Thinking* (New York: Little, Brown and Company, 2005).

Chapter 2

1. Karen Horney, *Our Inner Conflicts* (New York: Norton, 1945).

2. II Timothy 1:7 King James version.

3. Elias H. Porter, *Relationship Awareness Theory: Manual of Administration and Interpretation* (Carlsbad, CA: Personal Strengths Publishing, 1996).

4. Kenneth Blanchard, *The One-Minute Manager* (New York: William Morrow, 1982).

5. J. E. Ormrod, *Educational Psychology: Developing Learners* (Upper Saddle River, NJ: Pearson/ Merrill Prentice Hall, 2006).

6. Ed Bacon, *The Eight Habits of Love: Open Your Heart, Open Your Mind* (New York: Grand Central Life & Style, 2013). The eight habits are Generosity, Stillness, Truth, Candor, Play, Forgiveness, Compassion, and Community.

7. II Tim 1:7; Power (Against), Love (Toward), and Sound Mind (Away).

8. For example, Panache Desai, Dr. Deepak Chopra, Dr. Amit Goswami, Wayne Dyer, and Alan Wolf, to mention a few.

9. A quantum is a discrete quantity of energy proportional in magnitude to the frequency of the radiation it represents.

10. Daniel Goleman, Richard E. Boyatzis, and Annie McKee, *Primal Leadership: Learning to Lead with Emotional Intelligence* (Boston: Harvard Business Review Press, 2004).

11. Michael Singer, *The Untethered Soul: The Journey Beyond Yourself* (Oakland, CA: New Harbinger Publications, 2007).

12. This definition is taken from an introduction to an emotional intelligence 360 assessment developed by Kenneth M. Nowack, PhD, and released by Envisia Learnings © 2003 called

Emotional IntelligenceView360. Nowack gives us a concise summary of emotional intelligence's (EI) development for those readers interested when he states, "the most widely accepted model of EI has been influenced by several scientists and researchers. Howard Gardner's (1983) theory of multiple intelligences lists interpersonal and intrapersonal intelligence as unique and different from the mathematical/logical type recognized today as "IQ" or general intelligence. Peter Salovey and John Mayer first proposed their theory of EI in 1990 and Reuven Bar-On (1988) has placed EI in the context of health and well-being. Daniel Goleman (1998) formulated EI in terms of a theory of organizational and job performance."

13. Daniel Goleman, *Emotional Intelligence: Why It Can Matter More Than IQ* (New York: Bantam Books, 2005); *Working with Emotional Intelligence* (New York: Bantam Books, 2000); *Primal Leadership: Learning to Lead With Emotional Intelligence* (Boston: Harvard Business Review Press, 2004).

Chapter 3

1. For the rest of the book, the (+) sign before a dimension will indicate specifically the positive, energetic, above-the-line expression of that dimension. Likewise, the (–) sign will indicate

the negative, heavy, low-energy, below-the-line expression of that dimension.

2. Elias H. Porter, *Relationship Awareness Theory: Manual of Administration and Interpretation* (Carlsbad, CA: Personal Strengths Publishing, 1996).

3. Several excerpts from this section are taken from an earlier book, *Follow the Yellow Brick Road: How to Change for the Better When Life Gives You Its Worst.*

4. Robert Kaplan and Robert Kaiser "Rethinking a Classic Distinction in Leadership," *Consulting Psychology Journal* 55, no. 1 (2003).

Chapter 4

1. Saul McLeod, *Simple Psychology.* http://www.simplypsychology.org/carl-rogers.html.

2. www.CulturLogix.com.

3. The New International Version.

4. *Merriam-Webster's Collegiate Dictionary.*

5. Romans 12:15.

6. Sam Alibrando, *Follow the Yellow Brick Road: How to Change for the Better When Life Gives You Its Worst* (Bloomington, IN: iUniverse, 2007).

Chapter 5

1. H. Goldenberg and L. Goldberg, *Family Therapy: An Overview* (Boston: Thomas Brooks/Cole, 2007), 244, 467.

2. Darlene Lancer, *Codependency for Dummies* (New Jersey: John Wiley & Sons, Inc., 2012), 30.

3. 1 Corinthians 13: 1–8.

4. Ed Bacon, *The Eight Habits of Love: Overcome Fear and Transform Your Life* (New York: Grand Central Life & Style, 2012).

5. R. Meredith Belbin, *Management Teams* (Oxford, England: Butterworth-Heinemann, 1996).

6. Here are the nine roles: Plant (generator of ideas), Resource Investigator (networker, enthusiast), Coordinator (chairperson), Shaper (task-focused), Monitor-Evaluator (observer), Team-worker (the oil), Implementer (action), Completer-Finisher (perfectionist), and Specialist (content expert). You can see that all the roles circle the Relationship Circle. For example, the Team-worker is Blue and the Implementer is Red.

7. By Alan Sroufe and Daniel Siegel: http://www.drdansiegel.com/uploads/1271-the-verdict-is-in.pdf.

8. W. A. Spooner, "The Golden Rule." In *Encyclopedia of Religion and Ethics*, Vol. 6, edited by James Hastings, pp. 310–12. New York: Charles Scribner's Sons, 1914.,

9. For a good summary, I recommend reading her article at: http://www.dbtselfhelp.com/html/ radical_acceptance_part_1.html.

10. John 13: 1–17.

Chapter 6

1. Shunryu Suzuki in *Zen Mind, Beginner's Mind: Informal Talks on Zen Meditation and Practice*. Weatherhill (1970).

2. http://www.merriam-webster.com/dictionary/ aware.

3. From the lecture titled, "Practicing Presence: A Guide for the Spiritual Teacher and Health Practitioner," by Eckhart Tolle (c) 2003 (Eckhart Teachings, eckharttolle.com).

4. Daniel J. Siegel, "An Interpersonal Neurobiology Approach to Psychotherapy." *Psychiatric Annals*, April 2006.

5. To begin with just one article on the topic, you may appreciate: "7 Ways Meditation Can Actually Change the Brain," http://www.forbes. com/sites/alicegwalton/2015/02/09/7-ways-meditation-can-actually-change-the-brain/.

Chapter 7

1. Daniel Goleman, Richard E. Boyatzis, and Annie McKee. *Primal Leadership: Learning to Lead With Emotional Intelligence* (Cambridge: Harvard Business Review Press, 2004).

2. Please see the following white paper for more information on the good hire: http://apc3.com/d-i-s-c-o-the-good-hire-process/.

3. Multi-rater (or 360 degree) assessment is a survey that is given to the leader herself, her boss, people who work for her, her peers and sometimes her clients or vendors as well. In this way we get a "360 degree view" of the candidate. Often these surveys are normed so that you can compare this leader to thousands of other people who took the same survey.

4. Definition taken from our CulturLogix website: http://culturlogix.com/.

5. Like the Denison Organizational Culture Survey or the Global Culture Indicator.

6. Sam Alibrando, *Follow the Yellow Brick Road: How to Change for the Better When Life Gives You Its Worst* (Bloomington, IN: iUniverse, 2007).

Index

Absorption, 154-155

Abuse, 114

Acceptance, 177-178

Accumulated pain, 33-34

Acknowledgment, 166-167

Adapting, 54

Adaptive unconscious, 183

Adaptive, 186, 189, 208

Agency, 64, 165, 221

Agency, Power as, 110

Aggression, 134, 221

Agreeing, 23

Ainsworth, Dr. Mary, 149

Allowing, 177-178

Altruistic-Nurturing motivation, 58

Ambition, 121

Ambivalent attachment, 150

Analytic-Autonomizing motivation, 58

Anger management, 222

Anger, 129-130

Animal life, treatment of, 112-113

Anime, 161-162

Animus, 128

Annihilation, 194

Anxiety management, 222

Anxiety, 68, 81, 127, 160, 194, 204

Appease, 22, 23-24, 56

Appeasing, 23

Arguing, 22

Asocial tendencies, 192

Assertive-Directing motivation, 58

Assertiveness, 221

Attachment theory, 149

Attachment, 147-150

Automatic reactions, 40, 45-46

Avoidance, 93, 191

Avoidant attachment, 150

Awareness, 169-170, 175-177, 180, 187

Bacon, Ed, 68, 71, 144

Balance, 44-45, 73, 83-84, 167, 199-229

Baum, L. Frank, 33, 56, 170

Begley, Sharon, 145

Belbin, Meredith, 147, 223, 225

Belonging, 108

Benefits of meditation, 197

Best Self, 71

Biology, 58

Bion, Wilfred, 55, 58, 69

Blakemore, Sarah-Jayne, 142

Blame, 22, 124, 172

Blink, 46, 183

Blue, 62-66, 72, 75, 80, 84-85, 107, 108, 114, 115, 116, 117, 120, 126-127, 130, 133-167, 170, 180, 181, 184, 192, 193, 194, 199, 200, 221, 224, 225

Bowlby, John, 149

Brain stem, 45

Brain, emotional, 41

Brain, retraining the, 186-187

Breathing, 196

Calm, 187-188

Candor, 119-121

Capitalism, 117-118

Caring, 134

Challenges, 20

Change, resistance to, 46-49

Chemistry, relational, 207

Child, building a transcendent, 216-217

Codependence, 72, 89, 137

Cognitive-behavioral therapy (CBT), 58, 64

Coherent, 186, 189, 208

Collaboration, 143-147

Collaborative law, 146

Collective unconscious, 128, 161-162

Comeback, 30

Communication, 70

Compassion meditation, 145

Compassion, 145, 153-155, 197

Competition, 115-118, 144

Competitiveness, 221

Concern for others, 58

Confidence, 12

Confidence, 142

Conflict, 131

Conforming, 23

Confoundedness, 94, 129, 162-167, 195

Congregation, 143-147

Connecting, 69

Connection, 135-136

Conscious effort, 46

Consciousness, 175-177, 180

Containment, 165

Control, 58, 60

Convergence, 107-109, 134-138, 152, 170-174, 201

Cooperation, 143-147, 173-174

Coordination, 52

Cortex, 44-45

Courage, 118-119

Culture, organizational, 226-229

Darwin, Charles, 115-116

Dating, 205-208

Davidson, Dr. Richard, 144-145

Decisiveness, 221

Deep breathing, 196

Dependency, 63-64, 140-143

Depression, 163

Deprivation, 200

Depth, 52, 80

Destruction, 200

Detachment, 25, 89, 195-199

Determination, 12

Dharma, 71, 155

Dialectical behavior therapy (DBT), 158

Difficult people, 26-30

Dimensions of the interpersonal world, 51-77

Dimensions of the physical world, 52

Disassociation, 190

Disconnect, emotional, 23

Disconnection, 125, 139

Disengaged leadership style, 219

Disorganized attachment, 150

Divergence, 107-109, 134-138, 170-174, 201

Domain, 110

Dominion, 111

Eastern philosophies, 174

Effort, conscious, 46

Ego, 32-39, 70, 123, 125-126, 135, 142-143, 163, 172, 190, 192, 202, 203, 204, 210, 223, 233

Ego, pain-body and the, 30-39

Eight Habits of Love, The, 68, 144

Emotional brain, 41

Emotional disconnect, 23

Emotional health, 176

Emotional intelligence (EQ), 13, 73-75, 176, 186-187, 219, 220-222, 225

Emotional Life of Your Brain, The, 144

Emotional memories, 44

Emotion-notions, 33, 36, 40, 69, 161, 172, 190, 210, 233

Empathy, 125, 153-155, 221, 225

Enabling leadership style, 86-89, 219

Energetic, 186, 189, 208

Energy, vibrating, 135-136

Enmeshment, 136, 137

Envy, 125

Essential Self, 71

Evasion, 23

Evolution, 107

Exercise, 197

Experience, learning from, 183

Extraversion, 192

FACES, 185-187, 189, 208

Fear, 68, 93, 117, 202

Fear, ontological, 127-129, 160, 194

Fight, 22, 24, 25, 56

Flexible, 185, 189, 208

Flight, 22-23, 25, 56

fMRI, 142, 145

Follow the Yellow Brick Road, 11-12

Forceful leadership style, 86-89, 219

Freeze/Appease, 22, 23-24, 56

Freud, Sigmund, 68, 201

Frontal cortex, 45

Fulfillment, personal, 106

Gallese, Vittorio, 153

Gladwell, Malcolm, 46, 183-184

God-Self, 71

Golden Rule, the, 151-152

Goleman, Daniel, 37, 70, 73, 75, 220

Groups, Working the Triangle and, 94-96

Groupthink, 224, 225

Guilt, 172

Habit, 81

Haidt, Jonathan, 44

Happiness, 18-19, 106

Hate, 68, 123

Health, mental, 176

Heart Axis, 52

Heart, 12, 14, 20, 49, 52, 62-66, 72, 75, 80, 84-85, 107, 114, 115, 116, 117, 120, 126-127, 133-167, 170, 180, 184, 193, 194, 199, 200, 202, 234

Height, 52, 60, 80

Honesty, 40

Horney, Karen, 53-54, 58, 60, 62, 106, 171

Hostility, 22, 43

House of Cards, 122

Human attachment, 147-150

Human sweet spot, 202-204

Humiliation, 165

Humility, 165

Hypersensitivity, 137

Id, the, 201

Immaturity, 125

Immediate impulses, 201

Impatience, 22, 89

Importance, 58

Impulses, immediate, 201

Indifference, 25, 191-192

Inner tension, 53-54

Insecure attachment, 149

Insecurity, 126

Integration, 185-187

Intellectualization, 191

Intelligence, 62

Intensity, 40, 42-45

Interpersonal movement, 54-55

Interpersonal Triad, 49

Interpersonal Triangle Inventory (ITI), 14, 49, 76-77, 95, 225

Interpersonal Triangle, the, 49, 53-59, 75-76, 180, 202, 207, 212-213, 217, 222

Interpersonal Triangle, Working the, 79-103, 126-131, 159-160, 166-167, 193, 204-205, 215-216, 233

Introjects, 33

Introversion, 192

Intuition, 182-184

Joy, 17

Judgment, 30

Jung, Carl, 128, 161

Kaiser, Robert, 86

Kaplan, Robert, 86

Kindness, 173-174

Knowing, 55, 170-171, 172-173, 176, 182-184

Laughter, 37

Layering effect, 43-44

Leadership, 219-222

Leadership, EI and, 73-74

Leadership, resonant, 220

Learning from experience, 183

Least-preferred movement (LPM), 204, 206, 222

Length, 60

Limbic system, 26, 40-42, 44-45

Linehan, Dr. Marsha, 158

Listening, 221

Liveliness, 31

Love, 12, 55, 58, 72, 138-140

Mania, 163

Marriage, 209-213

Master Mode, the, 179-181

Mating, 205-208

Maturity, 74, 125, 208

Meditation, 145, 196-198

Memories, emotional, 44

Mental health, 176

Mind Axis, 52

Mindfulness meditation, 197

Mindfulness, 12, 14, 20, 49, 52, 62-66, 72, 74, 80, 84-85, , 106, 107, 114, 115, 116, 126-127, 160, 165, 169-178, 199, 201, 202, 234

Minuchin, Salvador, 136

Mirror neurons, 153-154

Miscommunication, 139

Monotheism, 173

Motivation, 43, 58

Movement, interpersonal, 54-55

Moving against, 58, 60, 80, 84-85, 105-131

Moving away, 58, 60, 80, 84-85, 169-198

Moving toward, 58, 60, 80, 84-85, 133-167

Moving-against solution, 54, 55

Moving-away solution, 54, 55

Moving-toward solution, 54, 55

Narcissism, 125, 154, 161

Narrative, rewriting our, 203

Natural selection, 116

Negative attitudes, 20

Neuroscience, 174

New Earth, A, 32

Nothingness, 194

Objectivity, 58

Observance, 107-109, 134-138, 170-174, 175-177

Observer, the, 171-172, 175

Ontological fear, 127-129, 160, 194

Organizational culture, 226-229

Origin of Species, The, 115

Our Inner Conflicts, 53

Ownership, 166-167

Pain, accumulated, 33-34

Pain-body, 30-39, 69, 123, 154, 161, 203, 210, 223, 233

Parenting, 213-219

Partnerships, 209-213

Passion, 12

People, difficult, 26-30

Perception, 42-45

Perseverance, 12

Physical strength, 198

Porter, Dr. Elias, 58, 82

Positivity, 70-71, 93

Power as agency, 110

Power Axis, 52

Power, 12, 14, 20, 49, 52, 58, 62-66, 72, 75, 80, 84-85, 105-131, 150, 160, 165, 170, 173, 184, 193, 199, 200, 202, 234

Presence, 177

Presence, the power of, 174, 175

Primal Leadership, 37, 220

Productivity, 70

Projection, 124

Prominence, 60

Psychological entities, unintegrated, 33

Psychology, 174

Radical Acceptance, 158-159

Random-access memory (RAM), 188-190

Reactive parenting, 213-216

Reactivity, 12, 17-50, 66, 190, 202, 233

Red, 62-66, 72, 75, 80, 84-85, 105-131, 134, 139, 140, 150, 159, 160, 163, 165, 170, 173, 181, 184, 193, 199, 200, 221, 223-224, 225

Reflection, 12

Relational chemistry, 207

Relational movements, 55

Relationship Awareness Theory, 58

Relationship Circle, the, 66-73, 74, 114, 126, 159, 193, 220

Relationship management, 73, 75

Resentment, 124

Resistance to change, 46-49

Resistance, 40

Resonant leadership, 220

Responsibility, 17-50, 141

Responsive parenting, 213-216

Retraining the brain, 186-187

Rewriting our narrative, 203

Rizzolatti, Giacomo, 153

Rogers, Carl, 108

Sacrifice, 155-157

Sadness, 163

Scientific function, 181-182

Secure attachment, 149

Self-acceptance, 29

Self-actualization, 108

Self-awareness, 29, 40, 73, 74

Self-control, 58, 65, 74, 169, 184-187, 201, 222, 225

Self-efficacy, 64

Self-hate, 28

Selfishness, 158

Self-love, 158

Self-management, 73, 74

Self-organization, 185

Self-protection, 122

Self-respect, 72

Self-sacrifice, 72, 119, 157

Sensitivity, 137-138

Service, 155-157

Shame, 172

Siegel, Daniel, 148, 184-185, 186

Signals, 42-45

Singer, Michael, 70, 71

Social awareness, 73, 75

Sociopaths, 200

Somatosensory cortex, 142

Spenser, Herbert, 116

Sroufe, Daniel, 148

Stability, 184-176

Stable, 186, 189, 208

Standing eave, 43-44

Stewardship, 111

Stillness, 187-188

Strength Deployment Inventory, 58

Strength, physical, 198

Subconscious, 46

Surrendering, 23

Survival of the fittest, 116

Sweet spot, 202-204

Sympathetic nervous system, 196

Synergy Pyramid, the, 89

Synergy, 84-89, 119-229

Teams, work, 222-226

Temper, 22

Tension, inner, 53-54

Thin-slicing, 183

Tolle, Eckhart, 32, 33, 69, 71, 123, 178

Tragedy, 18

Transcendent child, 216-217

Treatment of animal life, 112-113

True Self, 71, 233

Truth, 58, 120-121

Unconscious limbic system, 26

Unconscious, 46

Unconscious, adaptive, 183

Unconscious, collective, 128, 161-162

Unintegrated psychological entities, 33

Untethered Soul, The, 70

Versatile leadership style, 219

Vibrating energy, 135-136

Vulnerability, 162-163

Warmth, 60

Weakness, 142

Width, 52, 60, 80

Wisdom, 182-184

Withdrawal, 23

Witness Within, the, 171-172, 175

Wonderful Wizard of Oz, The, 56, 85, 110-111, 118, 161, 170, 179, 194-195

Work teams, 222-226

Working the Triangle, 79-103, 126-131, 159-160, 166-167, 193, 204-205, 215-216, 233

Xenophobia, 108-109

Yellow, 62-66, 72, 74, 80, 84-85, 106, 107, 114, 115, 116, 126-127, 130, 140, 145, 158, 160, 163, 165, 169-198, 199, 201, 222, 224, 225

Yielding, 23